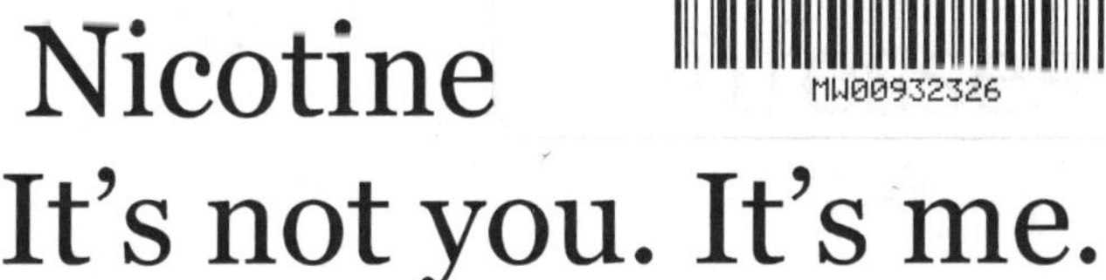

Nicotine
It's not you. It's me.

Joseph R DiFranza, M.D.
Illustrated by Amberlynn Narvie

First Print Edition. ISBN 978-1-105-57760-4

Table of Contents

Book 1: Nicotine Speaks: "It's not you. It's me."

Chapter 1	The Original Bug Zapper	5
Chapter 2	Your Brain's Day Job	7
Chapter 3	Who's In Charge?	11
Chapter 4	How I Hijack Your Brain	14
Chapter 5	Wanting, Craving, Needing	23
Chapter 6	Your Journey	27
Chapter 7	Nicotine Withdrawal	34
Chapter 8	Psychological Dependence	40
Chapter 9	Social Smokers	44
Chapter 10	What Happens When You Quit?	47

Book 2: Quitting Smart

Chapter 1	What's Wrong With You?	55
Chapter 2	What's Not Wrong With You?	57
Chapter 3	Nicotine Withdrawal	62
Chapter 4	Cold Turkey vs. Medication	66
Chapter 5	Know Your Enemy	72
Chapter 6	Your Game Plan	83
Chapter 7	Tapering: A Strategy to Avoid	98
Chapter 8	Stop Smoking Medicines	100
Chapter 9	Choosing Your Game Plan	114
Chapter 10	Snatching Defeat from the Jaws of Victory	125
Chapter 11	Benefits of Quitting	127
Chapter 12	Plan B	128

Appendix	The Health Hazards of Tobacco Use	132
	About the Author	136

Foreword

Nicotine addiction is a brain disease of nerves and chemicals, not a sign of a weak character. This book explains this brain disease in plain English. Each chapter in Book 1 should bring another "aha moment" as Nicotine confesses how it has controlled your brain since your first cigarette. Upon understanding that nicotine addiction is a disease and not a character flaw, smokers can rid themselves of the self-blame accumulated after countless failed attempts to cure their disease through will power. As Nicotine says: "It's not you. It's me." This book will make smokers feel better about themselves.

In Book 2, Dr. DiFranza discusses the tragically comical ways in which smokers unwittingly stack the odds against themselves when they decide to quit. Quitting smoking may be the hardest thing you will ever do. It's a fight you will lose unless you understand your enemy. Dr. DiFranza will provide you with state-of-the-art advice on how to give it your best shot. If you are looking for scary statistics, those are buried in the appendix because this book is not about frightening or lecturing smokers.

Modern medicine cannot cure every case of nicotine addiction. If you are one of those cases, Dr. DiFranza provides medical advice on how to give yourself the best chance of living a long and healthy life, while you continue to use nicotine. This book does not defend smoking, but it is sympathetic to the people who struggle with an addiction to nicotine and the people who love them.

Book 1
Nicotine Speaks: "It's not you. It's me."

Chapter 1
The Original Bug Zapper

Hi. My name is Nicotine and I think it is time that I come clean with you. I am responsible for addicting you and about a billion other people to tobacco. People make me out to be quite a villain, but by myself I am pretty harmless to people. I wasn't put on this earth to kill people; I was put here to kill bugs.

Once upon a prehistoric time, tobacco plants were getting eaten by bugs. A lucky genetic mutation in one tobacco plant gave it the ability to make me, Nicotine. The bugs that chewed on that plant keeled over and died. While the ordinary tobacco plants were devoured, the plant with the Nicotine mutation survived. Over the generations, the ordinary tobacco plants have died off and only the tobacco plants that make Nicotine have survived.

You might wonder why I kill bugs, but I don't kill the tobacco plant. Well the simple answer is that plants don't have brains. If you bear with me for just a minute, I will give you the technical answer and this is as technical as I am going to get.

Inside a bug brain the nerves talk to each other by releasing chemicals. The nerves have receptors on the outside as shown in the illustration on the next page. The receptors are like locks and the chemicals are like keys. The receptors have a particular shape and so do the chemicals. If the chemical fits in a receptor like a key fits in a lock, it can turn the nerve on or off.

A very important chemical in a bug's brain is called acetyl choline (AC). It turns out that I'm a dead ringer for AC. I'm an imposter, a counterfeit. I fit so well into the receptor for AC, that scientists call these receptors nicotinic receptors in my honor.

When a bug eats a tobacco plant with Nicotine in it, I get into the nicotinic receptors in the bug's brain. I turn on so many nerves at the same time that it fries that little bug brain. I am the original bug zapper. I am harmless to the tobacco plants since they have neither nerves nor brains. Humans, well that's another story. The human brain has so many nicotinic receptors that it is a mystery why people don't keel over dead the first time they smoke a cigarette.

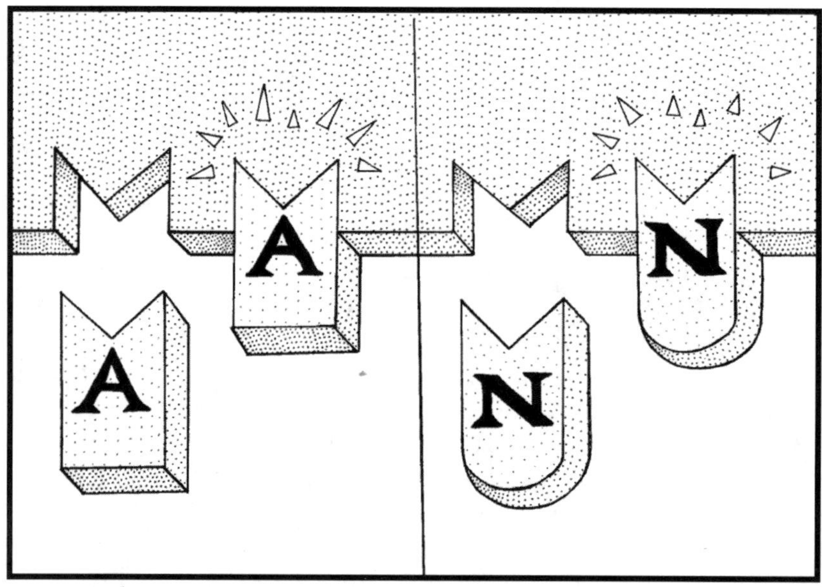

The left side of this illustration shows acetyl choline receptors and acetyl choline molecules. When the molecule slides into the receptor, the nerve is turned on. The right side of the illustration shows that the nicotine molecule can also slide into the receptor and turn the

Before I can tell you how I made you addicted, you need to understand a little bit about how your brain works. It turns out that thinking isn't your brain's day job.

Chapter 2
Your Brain's Day Job

Thinking is not your brain's day job. Your brain's main job is to keep you alive by keeping everything in your body in perfect balance. Every part of your body is connected to your brain. Your brain controls your metabolism by controlling your thyroid gland. The brain controls the heart rate, the rate of breathing, and the digestive system. By controlling your sex hormones, your brain controls the menstrual cycle and decides when you go through puberty and menopause. It even controls milk production in breast feeding mothers.

You are not aware of most of the ways in which your brain quietly keeps everything in order. But sometimes your brain needs your cooperation to make things right. When this happens, your brain controls your behavior without you even realizing it.

You could die if the level of sugar in your blood falls too low. Your brain keeps track of your sugar levels every minute of every day. When the brain senses a low sugar level, it will make you hungry so you will eat. It may increase the saliva in your mouth to help with digesting the food you will soon be eating. It is your brain, not your stomach that decides when you will feel hungry.

You can die from both dehydration and over hydration. So your brain keeps track of your hydration status every minute of every day and makes the proper adjustments to keep you alive. If your brain senses that you are getting dehydrated, it tells your salivary glands to make less saliva and your mouth gets dry. It signals the kidneys to save water and your urine turns yellow as the kidneys make the urine more concentrated. It also makes you thirsty so you will drink. If you drink too much, the brain signals the kidneys to get rid of water. Your kidneys make more urine and you might notice that it looks clear like water. It is your brain that decides when you are thirsty and how much urine your kidneys make.

You can die from being hypothermic (too cold) or hyperthermic (too hot). If your brain senses that you are becoming hypothermic, it will make you feel cold so that you bundle up. It might make your muscles shiver to generate heat to warm you up. If you are exercising and your brain senses that you are becoming hyperthermic it will make you feel hot so that you will shed clothing. It will signal the sweat glands to pour out sweat. The evaporating sweat cools your body.

When you have the flu, your brain raises your temperature. Doctors speculate that the brain raises and lowers your temperature when you are sick to kill the germs. When everyone else feels fine, your brain makes you feel cold so you will pile on the blankets. Your brain sends a signal to your muscles and you start to shiver involuntarily. Even though your temperature is 104 degrees, you have the chills and you feel like you are freezing. Then a few minutes later your brain decides that it wants to lower your temperature. It makes you feel hot. You throw off the blankets as you become drenched with sweat because your brain has turned on your sweat glands to cool you down. You do not get to decide whether you should feel hot or cold, whether you should shiver or sweat. Your brain is in control.

In addition to having sensors for sugar, hydration, and temperature, your brain has sensors for oxygen and carbon dioxide, the gases that you breathe in and out of your lungs. If you start to exercise, your muscles use up oxygen and produce carbon dioxide. Your brain senses this and makes you breathe faster. Ordinarily, you don't even think about your breathing. Your brain monitors the levels of oxygen and carbon dioxide in your blood every minute of every day and sends a signal to your chest every time it wants you to take a breath.

To keep your house at the right temperature, your house has a simple brain called the thermostat. In the winter, when the house gets too cool, the thermostat turns the furnace on. When the house warms up to the proper temperature, the thermostat turns the furnace off. In the summer, when the house gets too hot, the thermostat turns the air conditioner on. When the house cools down to the proper temperature, the thermostat turns the air conditioner off. Your brain works the same way. With all of its sensors it keeps track of everything that is going on in the body and continuously makes adjustments to keep everything at the proper setting. This is called **homeostasis**, when everything is at the proper setting and everything is in proper balance. By keeping everything in homeostasis, your brain keeps you alive. That is why creatures have brains. Thinking is just frosting on the cake.

Here is something to think about: while your brain is keeping everything else in your body at the proper setting, what is keeping your brain in proper adjustment? Your brain is made up of trillions of individual nerves and each nerve

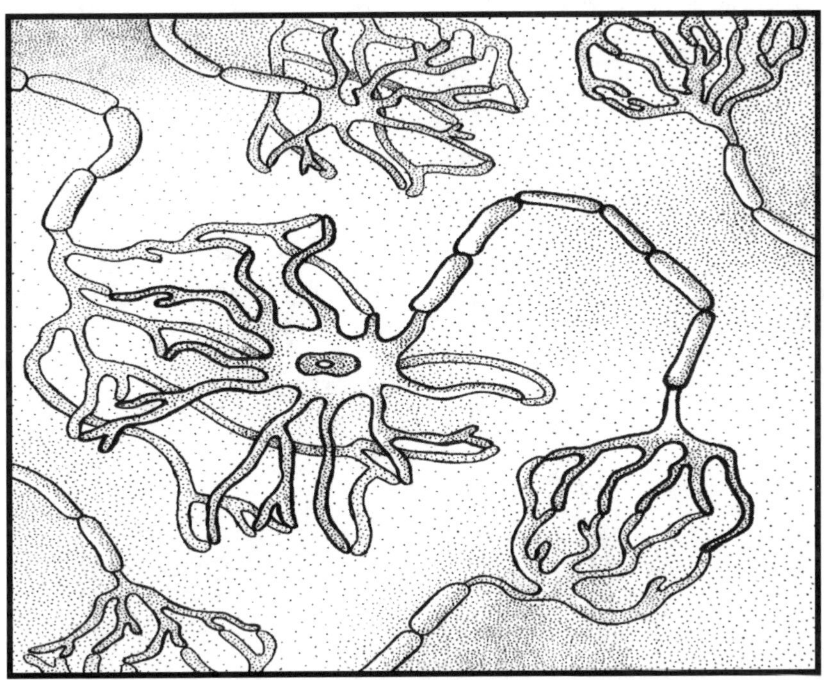

must be maintained at the proper level of excitability. It wouldn't do if a nerve was too lethargic, or too excitable. So the nerves have many different ways to adjust themselves so that they stay at the proper setting. They can make more connections with their neighbors, or they can break connections. They can make more receptors, or fewer receptors. They can change the types of receptors they have. They can change the balance of chemicals inside themselves. The nerves are blessed with many different ways in which they can adjust themselves to keep their level of excitability at the proper setting to keep the brain as a whole functioning properly.

Ironically, it is the brain's amazing capacity to repair itself that makes it so easy for me to get people addicted.

Chapter 3
Who's In Charge?

Since the part of the brain that keeps everything in homeostasis developed long before the thinking part of the brain, scientists sometimes call this the primitive brain. Here, primitive means coming first, not crude and clumsy.

I want you to notice that whenever your primitive brain wants you to do something, it gets you to do it by making you uncomfortable. It makes you feel hot. It makes you feel cold. It makes you hungry. It makes you thirsty. It makes you sleepy. You then exercise your free will to make yourself comfortable again. You eat. You drink. You put more clothes on, or you take them off. You get some sleep. While you are deciding to do all of these things, it is really your primitive brain that is calling the shots by making you uncomfortable in the first place. Since you need to do all of these things to keep yourself healthy, there is no reason for you to battle your primitive brain. You do what you need to do to get comfortable and that keeps you healthy.

But what if, like some science fiction movie plot, your primitive brain became convinced that it needs Nicotine to keep you alive? Then it would be making you do something that is unhealthy, that could even kill you. But I am getting ahead of myself here.

Most people believe that the thinking part of the brain is in complete control of their actions. But is it the thinking part of your brain, or the primitive part of your brain that is really in control? Let's do an experiment on you.

The primitive part of your brain allows the thinking part of your brain to have some control over when you inhale and exhale. This is because you need to control your breathing in order to swallow, to talk, and to dive under water. The fact that you can inhale and exhale at will makes it feel like the thinking part of your brain is in control of your breathing. If you want to see who is in control of your breathing, try holding your breath for two minutes. This will set up a battle of wills between your thinking brain and your primitive brain.

Take a deep breath and hold it until you finish reading this paragraph. After several seconds your brain will detect changes in the carbon dioxide level in your blood. It will send a signal to your chest to breathe. Use your thinking brain to resist the urge to breathe. Your primitive brain will send a stronger signal to your chest and you will have to exert an effort to prevent yourself from breathing. Now you are in a real battle of wills, your primitive brain is commanding your chest to breathe and your thinking brain is commanding it not to. Now your primitive brain can use a little psychological warfare. Just like your brain can make you feel thirsty, hungry, hot or cold, it can make you feel "air hunger." It can make you feel like you are suffocating long before you are in any jeopardy. You will feel the sensation that something is wrong inside your chest. You will feel the pressure building. You will feel such an urgent, intense and overwhelming desire to breathe that you can no longer resist.

As soon as you take a breath, these sensations go away instantly, before there is any change in the oxygen or carbon dioxide in your blood. The sensation goes away instantly because it was all in your head. Holding your breath causes no strain on your chest or lungs, those sensations were all in your head. Your primitive brain made you feel like you were about to die if you didn't take a breath. If your primitive brain senses that there is something wrong, it will do what it needs to do to control your behavior. You cannot kill yourself by holding your breath because your primitive brain will always win this battle of wills.

While we are on the subject of the primitive brain, it would be helpful to point out that many of the sensations that people have when they feel they need Nicotine are very similar to the sensations that the primitive brain uses when it wants you to eat, drink and breathe. Some smokers describe their need for Nicotine as being hungry, but for Nicotine instead of food. They feel an emptiness in the pit of the stomach. Some say that when they need Nicotine, they get extra saliva in their mouth, like when they are hungry. Others say their mouth feels dry like they are thirsty. Some smokers describe their need for Nicotine as a feeling that something is missing in their chest. Many smokers say that when they try to stop smoking they feel an urgent, intense need for Nicotine. They may feel a little panicky. It is no coincidence that the sensations that people feel when they need Nicotine are very similar to the sensations of hunger, thirst, and air hunger. When the primitive brain feels that Nicotine is key to your survival, it will make you feel uncomfortable however it can to get you to smoke.

Chapter 4
How I Hijack Your Brain

Until a few years ago, doctors thought that I was so weak that a person would have to smoke lots of cigarettes everyday for years before I could cause addiction. But that all changed when a young teenage girl told Dr. DiFranza that she was already addicted after smoking one pack. It turned out this girl was not unusual. Lots of teens who had smoked only a few cigarettes were already showing symptoms of addiction. Soon doctors discovered that they had underestimated my powers and pretty much everything they had assumed about me was wrong. Now that my secret is out, it would be my pleasure to explain exactly how I got you addicted, and how I keep you addicted.

When cigarettes were cheap, some people smoked two or more packs per day. Scientists figured that if some people had to smoke 40 or more cigarettes per day to satisfy themselves, the Nicotine in one cigarette must have very little effect on the brain. How wrong they were!

When teens reported symptoms of addiction after smoking only a few cigarettes, scientists started to look at the effect that one cigarette can have on the brain. They were shocked. The brain has billions or trillions of nicotinic receptors. The Nicotine in two puffs on a cigarette is enough to fill half of the nicotinic receptors in the brain. Smoking one cigarette fills 88% of the receptors. So it turns out that one cigarette is all it takes to get the job done. It was no longer a mystery how the Nicotine from one cigarette could affect the brain, the mystery was why some people need to smoke two packs per day when one cigarette fills 88% of their nicotinic receptors. I will explain that later.

Another way scientists went wrong is that they assumed that the effect I have on the brain stops as soon as I leave. Can you still remember how the Nicotine from your first cigarette made you feel? You might have felt lightheaded or dizzy. Or maybe you felt a good buzz as I turned on all of those nerves in your brain. Most people say that the head rush they got from smoking the first few times lasted less than a minute, maybe only a few seconds. If you managed to keep the smoke down in your lungs long enough, you might have experienced an overdose with just a few puffs. I would have made you feel like you were about to lose your lunch. Anything you felt, good or bad, would have been gone within minutes, leaving you to wonder what was all the fuss about smoking? Common sense would have told you that any effect I had was like a flash in the pan, over in a few seconds.

Scientists thought that my effect on the brain worked like the key to your car. You put the key in and turn it, and your engine starts. You take the key out, and the engine stops immediately. When you take a drag on a cigarette I reach your brain in 14 seconds. When you snub out your cigarette, the Nicotine levels in your blood start to fall immediately. Within 2 hours, only half of the Nicotine remains, after 4 hours only one quarter remains, and after 6 hours only one eighth remains. Twenty four hours after you snub out your cigarette, there is essentially no Nicotine left in your body.

Scientists thought that I could only cause addiction if you kept a lot of Nicotine in your brain all day long. In other words, they thought that you had to keep the motor revving all day long to get addicted. They also thought that to keep the motor running, you would have to light up a cigarette every 3 hours during the day.

What the scientists failed to take into account is that when I turn on the nerves that have nicotinic receptors, those nerves release their own chemicals like dopamine, serotonin, GABA, and noradrenaline. In a chain reaction, these chemicals turn on and off other nerves that remain on or off long after Nicotine is gone. When Nicotine turns on nerves it is like pushing over the first domino. Once the second domino falls, you can remove the first domino but that won't stop all of the other dominos from falling. Although one dose of Nicotine is completely gone from the body in less than 24 hours, one dose of Nicotine changes the concentration of crucial chemicals in your brain for at least a month! It turns out that many of the effects I have on the brain can last at least a month after one dose.

Now you know that the Nicotine from one cigarette is enough to fill billions of nicotinic receptors in your brain, turning on billions of nerves with effects that can last up to a month. So how does that cause addiction?

Remember, that the brain's main job is to keep everything, including itself, operating at the proper settings. You might say that the brain is a little obsessive-compulsive in that it spends all day and all night checking and rechecking everything. So when I enter the brain masquerading as acetyl choline (AC) and turn on billions of nerves that are not supposed to be on, it gets your brain's attention. When those nerves turn on other nerves and cause the release of chemicals like dopamine, noradrenaline, serotonin and GABA, that also gets your brain's attention. It is like I cause a massive short circuit in your brain, while you feel only a brief head rush or nothing at all.

Since I am causing all sorts of havoc, the nerves in the brain immediately start to adjust themselves to counteract my effects and restore everything back to their proper levels. Some of these counter measures are almost instantaneous, while others may take weeks to develop. For example, in less than a second, the nicotinic receptors deactivate themselves so that I can no longer stimulate them. But this does nothing to fix the damage as the dominos are already falling. One nerve stimulates another and another in a chain reaction.

As I said before, many of the effects I have can last up to a month, so the brain has a lot of work to do to counter these effects. Very recently scientists discovered that one dose of nicotine is enough to activate hundreds of different genes in the brain. They don't know exactly what these particular genes do, but genes are the blueprints for the parts that make up a nerve and allow it to function. The fact that I activate hundreds of genes suggests that the nerves are activating a number of different mechanisms to restore themselves to their proper settings. Within one day, the nerves have already increased the number of nicotinic receptors, probably to replace the receptors that were deactivated. So when you snuck your first cigarette you set off a chain reaction in your brain. By the next day, your nerves were pumping out chemicals, they were scrambling to make new receptors, and activating genes to make new parts. This is how addiction can start with the first cigarette.

In your brain there are nerves that are responsible for making you crave things. Hunger and thirst are forms of craving. Craving is your brain's way of getting you to do something.

Your brain also needs a way to stop the craving when you have eaten enough, or drank enough. So there are other nerves that act like a brake on craving. These nerves shut off the craving and make you feel satisfied and content. The figure illustrates this using a balance scale. On one side, there are nerves that make you crave and on the other side there are nerves that make you feel satisfied.

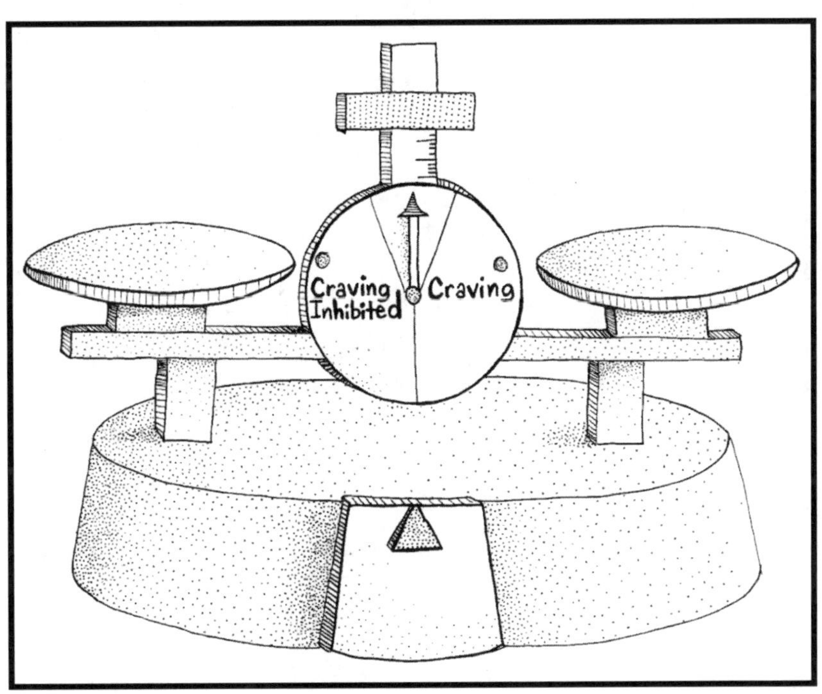

As shown in the next figure, I activate the nerves that make you feel satisfied. By activating the satisfaction nerves, I put the brakes on craving.

I can take away your craving for food. Smoking after a meal can make you feel even more satisfied. When all of your needs feel satisfied, you feel content and relaxed, everything is OK. Advertisements for Parliament promise “the satisfaction you seek.” Nicotine won’t get you high, but I can make you feel relaxed and satisfied.

I guess if I have a fault it is that I am just too much of a good thing. When I make you satisfied the brain realizes that things are out of balance. The brain counters my effects by making the necessary **Adaptations** to put things back in balance. This is illustrated in the next figure by the Adaptation mechanic who stands on the other side of the balance.

As the figure shows, the brain's Adaptations counteract my effect and craving and satisfaction are back in balance.

But what happens when the Nicotine effect wears off? That is shown in the next figure. When my effect wears off, the Adaptations throw everything off balance in the opposite direction. This causes craving.

The brain cannot undo the Adaptations, so it needs Nicotine to put things back in balance. Just as the brain makes you hungry or thirsty in order to restore homeostasis, it makes you crave nicotine in order to restore homeostasis.

As shown in the figure, when you smoke another cigarette, I stop the craving, and you feel relieved and satisfied, for a while.

To your brain, Nicotine may seem just as essential to your health and survival as oxygen, food and water. All are needed to keep your brain functioning at the proper set points. The brain can't make its own oxygen, food and water, so it makes you get them. The brain can't get its own Nicotine, so it makes you get it. Just as your brain makes you feel uncomfortable in order to get you to eat, drink and breath, it makes you uncomfortable in order to get you to smoke a cigarette. The craving you feel for Nicotine may feel like the sensations of hunger, thirst or air hunger, because these are the ways your brain knows it can get you to deliver the goods.

Some smokers say that they hated their first cigarette, but for some reason, a few days later they were craving another one. Your need for Nicotine has nothing to do with pleasure or self indulgence. It has everything to do with maintaining the homeostasis of your brain.

Most scientists still think that Nicotine works like a car key. You put the key in and the engine starts, you take the key out and the engine stops. But a better analogy would be you put the key in and the engine starts. You pull out of your driveway and a police cruiser pulls up behind you. Knowing that you have had your license suspended for 20 unpaid parking violations, you step on the gas. You lead the police on a high speed chase through town. You side swipe a row of parked cars, lose control of your car, knock over a fire hydrant and plow through a plate glass window into the lobby of a bank. You take out the key and the engine stops. Although the engine has stopped, you will be living with the repercussions of the past few minutes for a long time to come. Because Nicotine triggers irreversible changes in your brain, you may be living with the consequences for many years to come. I am like a tsunami that hits your brain: nothing may be the same again.

Chapter 5
Wanting, Craving, Needing

When you first get addicted, the cravings are mild and infrequent. When the effects of Nicotine wear off and the craving nerves get excited you feel only a mild desire to smoke. Smokers often call this mild desire **wanting**. It is like getting the urge to eat chocolate or some other food that you like. If you can easily get a cigarette you will smoke it, but you are not going to drop what you are doing to go find one. The urge to smoke is mild and you can ignore it. Even if you don't try to ignore it, it will go away after a few minutes. This wanting, a mild desire to smoke that is easily ignored, is the first symptom of addiction. But smokers don't know that.

When wanting starts, it may come only once a week or maybe just once a month. Since wanting is not strong enough to make you go out of your way for a cigarette, smokers with wanting usually only smoke when they are hanging out with friends who smoke. Then they can bum cigarettes from their friends.

When you first develop Wanting, you are in the first stage of Nicotine addiction. People often remain in first stage of addiction for a year or two. But each additional cigarette they smoke makes the addiction stronger. With each cigarette, the brain puts up more counter measures. The stronger the counter measures, the greater the craving when my effect wears off. Over time, your addiction grew stronger and you entered the second stage of addiction, **Craving**.

In the second stage of addiction, when my effect wears off, the excited craving nerves cause a stronger desire to smoke that most smokers call craving. Craving is a stronger desire to smoke than wanting. Craving lasts longer than wanting. It is harder to ignore. It may interrupt your thoughts, making it hard to concentrate on what you are doing. Whereas Wanting would not make you go out of your way for a cigarette, Craving might. With Craving you can wait to finish what you are doing and then go for a cigarette.

Some smokers say that when they have Craving it feels like their brain is telling them that it is time for a cigarette.

Some say that craving is a mental sensation, while others say it is a physical sensation, like hunger, only for Nicotine instead of food. They feel an emptiness in their stomach. Some smokers feel their mouth fill with saliva as if they were about to eat something. Other smokers experience a dry mouth, like their brain is trying to make them thirsty. Some smokers say that Craving feels like something is missing inside their chest, like you might experience with air hunger. Others say that Craving feels like something is missing from their blood. Through these symptoms your brain is making you feel uncomfortable so that you will smoke so it can get the Nicotine it needs to restore homeostasis.

In the second stage of addiction, when a smoker goes too long without smoking, first they will experience Wanting. If they ignore the Wanting, it will go away, but after a while the Craving will appear. Craving is unpleasant and difficult to ignore.

With each additional cigarette the addiction grows stronger as the brain puts up stronger Adaptations. The stronger the counter measures, the greater the craving when my effect wears off. Over time, the smoker enters the third stage of Nicotine addiction: **Needing**.

In the third stage of addiction, when you go too long without smoking, you will first experience Wanting. If your brain doesn't get the Nicotine it needs, it will make you feel Craving. If it still doesn't get the Nicotine it needs, it will hit you with Needing.

Smokers describe Needing as an intense and urgent desire to smoke. It can't wait. Some people call this a Nicotine fit. The need to smoke is so intense that it is impossible to ignore. You can't concentrate on anything but your need for a cigarette. Some people feel panicky. You will drop whatever you are doing and go for a smoke. You will go out in a blizzard for a smoke if you have to. If you run out of cigarettes, you will light up a stale butt from the ashtray. Or you will drive to the convenience store late at night in your pajamas.

Wanting will go away easily if ignored. Craving is harder to ignore, but it will eventually go away. Needing won't go away if you try to ignore it. You feel terrible and can't function right, and you know that you won't be able to function right and feel normal again until you have a cigarette.

By now you should be able to figure out what stage of addiction you are in, Wanting, Craving or Needing.

Stages of addiction
No Addiction You can stop using tobacco for weeks at a time and it doesn't bother you. You have no withdrawal symptoms when you stop smoking.
Stage 1-Wanting Whenever you go too long without smoking you notice a mild desire to smoke that will go away in a short time if you ignore it. It isn't hard to ignore.
Stage 2-Craving Whenever you go too long without smoking the desire for a cigarette becomes so strong that it interrupts your thoughts and is hard to ignore.
Stage 3-Needing Whenever you go too long without smoking you feel an urgent need to smoke. The desire to smoke is so urgent that it is hard to concentrate on anything else. You feel that you won't be able to feel and function right until you smoke again.

Although this is hard for me to say, you did not get addicted because you fell in love with me and the pleasure of smoking. Nor did you get addicted to me because you have a weak character, or an addictive personality. You got addicted because I hit your brain like a tsunami and your brain had to counter my effects in order to restore homeostasis. You got addicted because your brain cannot function normally without me. Just like your brain regulates your oxygen levels and sugar levels to keep itself in balance, it now regulates your nicotine levels to keep itself in balance. Just as your brain can make you hungry, or make you feel panicky if you hold your breath too long, it can make you hungry for

Nicotine and make you feel panicky if you go too long without it. It's like your brain thinks you need Nicotine to stay alive. Just like your brain will not allow you to hold your breath until you die, it will do everything it can to keep you smoking.

In the second part of this book, Dr. DiFranza will help you out of this predicament. But first, I have a lot more to tell you about how I have controlled your behavior since that first cigarette. I'm not gloating. Well maybe a little, but the more you know about my tricks, the better your chances of breaking free from your addiction.

Chapter 6
Your Journey

There are two main reasons why people try that first cigarette: curiosity and image. With a billion smokers on the planet, young people wonder what those people get out of smoking. Smokers are willing to stand out in the blazing sun on the hottest day of the year, or stand out in a blizzard on the coldest day of the year to smoke. Smoking must be the best thing ever. Kids don't realize that 80% of smokers wish they had never started.

Automobiles are the only consumer product that is more heavily advertised than cigarettes. Cigarette ads promised you that cigarettes were the answer to every adolescent insecurity. They would make you attractive, mature, independent, and popular. A lot of kids start smoking to fit into a group of kids that are already smoking, hoping that smoking will bring them acceptance.

Whatever the reason was for you trying your first cigarette, chances are that you didn't enjoy it. When nonsmokers are given Nicotine through a vein, most find it to be an unpleasant experience. Only one out of five people report that they liked their first cigarette. Most hated the taste and the burning irritation. Kids who try smoking out of curiosity usually find that smoking one cigarette is enough to satisfy their curiosity and they decide that they don't like it. So if your goal is to get kids addicted to smoking, you don't want to rely on curiosity alone.

For most people it seems I am an acquired taste. In fact, the more addicted you get, the more pleasurable I am. The trick is to get kids to smoke long enough for the addiction to take hold. That is where advertising can help. If you can get kids to stick with smoking because they are convinced it will make them attractive, mature, independent, and popular, it won't be long before they are addicted. While the changes in the brain start with the first dose of nicotine, most people are not addicted after smoking one cigarette. About half of smokers are addicted by the time they have smoked 20 cigarettes, and 95% are addicted by the time they have smoked 100 cigarettes.

It takes only one cigarette to addict some people, and others, it takes 100. Genetics explains why some people get addicted faster than others. Different people react to me differently. For example, only one in five people get a feeling of relaxation from their first cigarette, but these are the people who are at the highest risk of addiction.

Scientists used to think that your brain was fully grown when you were born, but now they know that the brain is not fully developed until a person is 25 years old. The younger a person is, the faster their brain is growing. Just like young people learn new languages much faster than adults, a young person's brain adapts to Nicotine quicker. Since it is the brain's Adaptation to Nicotine that causes the addiction, the younger a person is when he or she starts to smoke, the stronger the addiction will be. Adults who started smoking in junior high school are usually more addicted than those who started in high school. They are heavier smokers and have a harder time quitting.

So let's go back to when you started smoking. When you started to experience Wanting, you wouldn't know that Wanting is a sign of addiction and you would think that you smoked only because you enjoyed smoking. The Wanting would feel just like any other desire you might have, for example, wanting potato chips or candy. To you, the fact that you wanted a cigarette was just proof that you had acquired a taste for smoking.

When the Wanting stage of addiction started, you may have only been smoking one cigarette per month. When the Wanting stage starts, my effects could last a month or more. That means that smoking one cigarette would restore homeostasis in your brain for a whole month. After a month, your brain would make you want to smoke another cigarette. You may have smoked one cigarette, then hung out with your friends while they smoked every day for the next month, and then one day, out of the blue, you felt the urge to smoke again. After smoking that cigarette, you might not have had the urge to smoke again for several weeks. A lot of people in the Wanting stage smoke only at parties, or only when they are drinking. They don't buy cigarettes. They bum them off their friends.

When people are in the Wanting stage of Nicotine addiction they do not even think of themselves as smokers because they don't smoke every day, they don't feel bad when they go without smoking for several days, they never feel a need to smoke, they have never bought their own cigarettes, and they intend to stop smoking before they get addicted. They are already addicted and don't even think that they are smokers. Am I sneaky, or what?

If people were able to smoke just one cigarette per month forever, instead of a million people dying from smoking every year, it would be more like a thousand, and nobody would be on my case. Unfortunately for me, once addiction starts the ball rolling there's no stopping it.

I explained in the last chapter how each cigarette makes the addiction stronger as Wanting turns into Craving and then into Needing. There is one more thing you need to understand. When you first started to smoke my effects would last up to a month. I call that the **Latency**. The Latency is how long the Nicotine in one cigarette can keep the brain in homeostasis. After a Latency of one month, my effect wears off and the brain goes out of balance. As you smoke more cigarettes, the brain builds more Adaptations and the Latency gets shorter. In other words, my effect wears off sooner. Instead of keeping everything in the brain homeostatic for one month, smoking one cigarette may keep things in balance for only one week.

Why is this important? Well, this explains how you got from your first cigarette to where you are today. At first you might have smoked only one cigarette per month when your brain made you feel Wanting. As your Latency shortened to one week, you would feel the Wanting more often. Many kids start by smoking about once per month or less. Then they are smoking once per week, usually at parties on weekends. As the Latency shortens to a few days, they begin to smoke during the week also, usually after school with their friends. Each time the Wanting prompts you to smoke another cigarette, the addiction gets a little stronger and the Latency a little shorter.

Each additional cigarette brings you a little closer to the Craving stage of addiction. Kids usually reach the Craving stage when they are only smoking a few cigarettes per week. Remember that Craving is stronger than Wanting, and is harder to ignore. Wanting is a pleasant feeling. It is like looking at a desert and thinking "that looks good." Craving, on the other hand, is kind of unpleasant, like being really hungry. It doesn't feel good to be really hungry. When you are really hungry, you will eat food that is not particularly appealing just to take the hunger away. When you are craving a cigarette, you will go out of your way for a cigarette just to make the craving stop. You might smoke a brand that tastes awful. When smokers get to the Craving stage, for the first time in their life they feel uncomfortable when they can't smoke.

If smokers in the Craving stage of addiction go too long without a cigarette, they will first feel Wanting, then the Wanting will intensify into Craving. So there is a Latency to Wanting, and a longer Latency to Craving. As you expose your brain to Nicotine over and over, both the Latency to Wanting and the Latency to Craving shorten. The Latency to Craving puts an outside limit on how far apart you can space your cigarettes and still feel comfortable.

The Latency to Craving limits how far apart you can comfortably space your cigarettes, but there is nothing to say that you have to wait until you feel Craving to smoke. People enjoy lighting up after a meal, while they are talking on the phone, when they are drinking, and when they are bored. Kids like to smoke when they are hanging out with their friends. I call these **Elective** cigarettes. Your brain is not requiring you to smoke these cigarettes. You are actually smoking these cigarettes just because you want to, not because your brain is telling you to.

Each time you smoke an Elective cigarette, it restores the homeostatic balance in your brain. If you think of the Latencies as an alarm clock that tells you when you have to smoke, Elective cigarettes are like hitting the snooze button. When you smoke an Elective cigarette, it resets the timer on your Latencies. Every cigarette you smoke resets the timer on your Latencies.

Say you have a Latency to Craving of two days which means you would only experience Craving if you went two days without smoking. If you smoked a cigarette on Monday, then you would not expect to feel Craving until Wednesday. But what if you went ahead and smoked an Elective cigarette on Tuesday? That would reset the Latency to Craving and you would not expect to feel Craving until Thursday. And if you went ahead and smoked an Elective cigarette on Wednesday, you would postpone the Craving until Friday. In fact, if your Latency to Craving was two days and you smoked every day, you wouldn't experience Craving at all. It's like the old song, "How can I miss you if you won't go away?"

Because of the cigarettes smoked as Elective cigarettes and those that are smoked because of Wanting, many smokers in the Craving stage of addiction experience Craving only on occasions when they do not have the opportunity to smoke. For teens, this is usually a trip with their parents.

When smokers reach the Craving stage of addiction, they are usually smoking several days per week, but not every day. At first their Latency to Craving may be three days. It shortens gradually to two days, then to one day. It may take a year or two from starting to smoke to having a Latency to Craving of one day.

Before the Latency to Craving shortens to one day, most smokers get their cigarettes by stealing them from their parents' packs or bumming them off their friends. When the Latency to Craving gets down to one day, the smoker cannot skip smoking for a day without feeling uncomfortable. Once they realize this, smokers want a more reliable source of cigarettes so they don't run out. Once the Latency to Craving shortens to one day, most smokers will buy their own cigarettes for the first time.

It is usually at this point that the smoker starts to think of themselves as a smoker for the first time because they are smoking every day and buying their own cigarettes. However, they still do not think they are addicted because they do not have to smoke a pack every day like other people they know.

When the Latency to Craving is one day, the smoker must smoke at least one cigarette every day to remain comfortable. But with Elective cigarettes, most smokers at this stage might smoke two or three cigarettes per day. With each cigarette smoked, whether it is a required cigarette, or an Elective cigarette, the addiction grows stronger and the Latency to Craving shortens a little more.

The Craving stage of addiction is followed by the Needing stage. When people in the Needing stage try to go without smoking, they will first feel Wanting, then Craving, and then Needing. The experience of Needing is so nasty that smokers in the Needing stage try their best not to let themselves get to the point of Needing. They smoke as soon as they get to Wanting or Craving. So it is the Latency to Craving that determines how long smokers in both the Craving and Needing stages can remain comfortable without smoking.

The Latency to Craving of one day gradually shortens to 18 hours, to 12 hours, to 8 hours, and to 6 hours. When your Latency to Craving has shortened to 6 hours, you may feel a strong craving for a cigarette the minute you wake up in the morning because it has been more than 6 hours since your last cigarette. When the Latency to Craving shortens to 6 hours it is hard to get through the work day and smokers will be sure to smoke before going into work to reset the Latency to Craving so they can make it to lunch when they can go out for a smoke.

When the Latency to Craving shortens to less than 6 hours, kids will have a hard time getting through the school day without smoking. They will be sure to smoke a cigarette before school. Kids learn how long their Latency to Craving is because they notice which period they are in when the Craving starts to make it hard to concentrate on school work. They struggle to ignore the Craving, but Craving is hard to ignore. When their Latency to Craving is shorter than the school day, kids will sneak a quick Nicotine fix in the school bathroom, or out by the dumpster. Their teachers sneak out to their cars for a quick fix.

When the Latency to Craving shortens to an hour, a person would have to smoke every hour to remain comfortable throughout the day. Most people are awake for 16 hours per day, so a Latency to Craving of one hour would require one to smoke 16 cigarettes. With a few Elective cigarettes thrown in, that would come out to one pack per day. When the Latency to Craving is one hour, people have trouble sitting through a long movie or church service.

In some unfortunate people, the Latency continues to shorten. When it shortens to 30 minutes, smokers may have to smoke a pack and a half per day. When it shortens to 20 minutes, they get up to two packs per day. In some really unfortunate people the Latency to Craving shortens to just a few minutes and they need to chain smoke to stay comfortable. People with really short Latencies may be awakened in the middle of the night by their need for Nicotine and smoke so they can go back to sleep.

So the shortening of the Latency explains how you got from smoking one cigarette, maybe once a month, to smoking whatever you need to smoke now. It was an automatic process. As your brain developed Adaptations to Nicotine, the Latencies shortened, and you had to smoke more and more often, just to keep the nerves in your brain functioning properly. If the Latencies didn't shorten, you and your brain might still be satisfied smoking one cigarette a month.

Chapter 7
Nicotine Withdrawal

Your brain makes you feel Wanting, Craving and Needing when my effects are wearing off. This is your brain's way of getting Nicotine when it needs it to stay in balance. Although doctors call these withdrawal symptoms, you don't have to stop smoking to have withdrawal symptoms. Every time you experience Wanting, Craving or Needing, you are experiencing a withdrawal symptom. Those people who have a Latency to Craving of only a few minutes may experience the withdrawal symptom of Craving dozens of times each day even though to their friends and family it seems that they are always smoking.

Some people have a Latency to Craving of 5 or 6 days, while others have a Latency to Craving of 5 or 6 minutes. It is not the level of Nicotine in your blood that determines when you feel a withdrawal symptom, it is the length of time that has passed since your last cigarette. It's all about the timing. People with a very short Latency to Craving will experience withdrawal symptoms even though they have very high levels of Nicotine in their blood from morning to night. People with a Latency to Craving of four days will experience no withdrawal symptoms for several days even though all of the Nicotine from their last cigarette was gone within 24 hours.

Wanting, Craving and Needing are not the only withdrawal symptoms. The craving nerves are not the only nerves that get out of balance if they go too long without Nicotine. I work on many different parts of your brain, and these other parts also come to need me to stay in balance. When deprived of Nicotine, many parts of your brain stop functioning right. If it has been too long since your last cigarette, your reaction time slows down. You are not as good at making quick decisions. You can't concentrate as well. These effects are not obvious and you might notice them only under demanding conditions, like playing video games where you need to think and act very quickly. Scientists have tested smokers when they are deprived of Nicotine. Whatever it is, from taking tests to driving a car, you do it worse when deprived of Nicotine.

Caffeine definitely improves your performance. It improves alertness and reaction times. Sadly to say, I must admit that I do not improve your performance on anything.

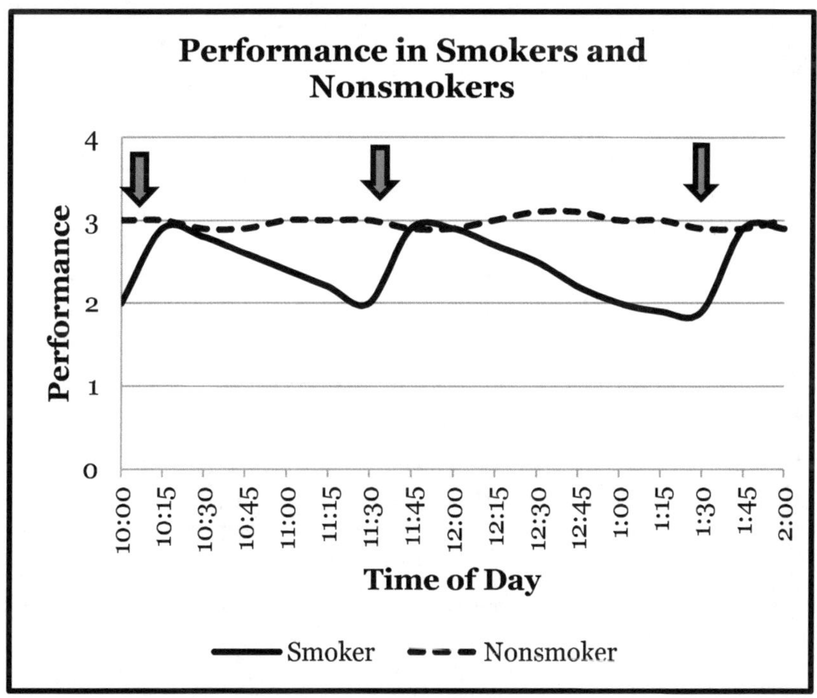

As shown in the figure, when smokers have their Nicotine, they perform the same as nonsmokers, not better. The arrows in the figure show when the smokers smoke a cigarette. After a cigarette, the performance in smokers is the same as in nonsmokers, but as withdrawal starts, their performance deteriorates. So it isn't that I make you function better, it is just that when you miss me your performance is worse.

There are also emotional withdrawal symptoms. When it has been too long since your last cigarette the nerves in the part of your brain that is in charge of emotions also get out of balance. What does that feel like? You feel the opposite of relaxed. You might feel anxious, restless and fidgety. You might feel irritable. Little things annoy you and you get angry over nothing. You have no patience. You may feel dissatisfied and depressed and may have trouble sleeping. People don't usually start to feel these emotional withdrawal symptoms until they get to the Craving or Needing stages of Nicotine addiction.

The table lists the most common symptoms of Nicotine withdrawal. It also lists common symptoms of stress. Nicotine withdrawal makes you feel stressed out.

Nicotine Withdrawal Symptoms	**Stress Symptoms**
Anxiety	Anxiety
Restlessness	Restlessness
Irritability	Irritability
Difficulty concentrating	Difficulty concentrating
Difficulty sleeping	Difficulty sleeping

If you have a long Latency, smoking a cigarette will keep the withdrawal symptoms away for a long time. If you have a short Latency, smoking a cigarette may make the withdrawal symptoms go away for only a few minutes, and then they are back. In either case, the longer you go without a cigarette the more stressed you feel.

The figure on the next page compares two smokers, one with a Latency of about one hour and the other with a Latency of 3 hours. The arrow shows that both smokers smoked a cigarette at 10 in the morning. The smoker with the shorter Latency is starting to feel Wanting by 11 AM and is Needing a cigarette by 1 PM. By 1 PM, the smoker with the longer Latency is just starting to feel Wanting and does not feel Needing until 5 o'clock.

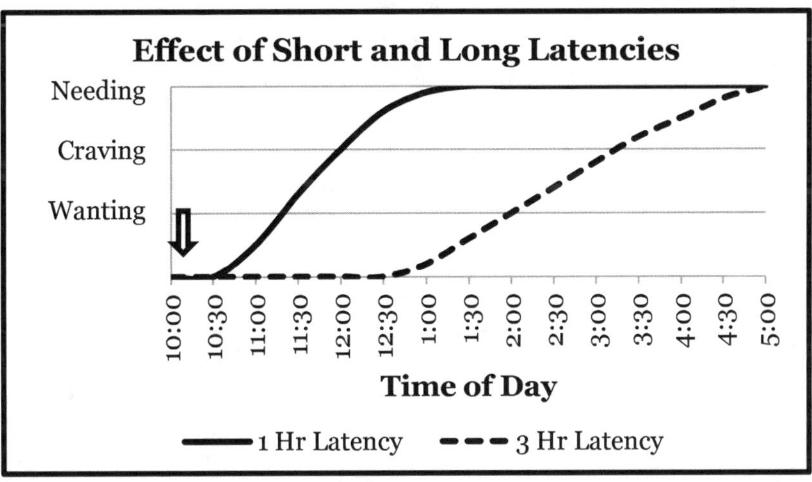

People smoke to help themselves deal with stress and to relax. What they don't realize is that most of their stress comes from nicotine withdrawal. Withdrawal makes stress levels climb as the effect of each cigarette wears off. Smoking a cigarette relieves these symptoms only temporarily. Smokers think that they are naturally full of stress and smoking helps them relax. In reality, the way they feel after smoking a cigarette is their real personality, and it is nicotine withdrawal that is making them feel stressed. Smoking doesn't do anything special for them, it just returns them to normal for a while. If they could stop smoking, they would usually feel like they do when they have just finished a cigarette.

The next figure shows stress levels in smokers compared to nonsmokers. The arrows show when the smoker has smoked a cigarette. Throughout the day, nicotine withdrawal increases the stress levels of smokers above that of nonsmokers. Smoking temporarily removes the stress of withdrawal, restoring the smoker to normal, but even immediately after smoking a cigarette, the smoker is not more relaxed than a nonsmoker.

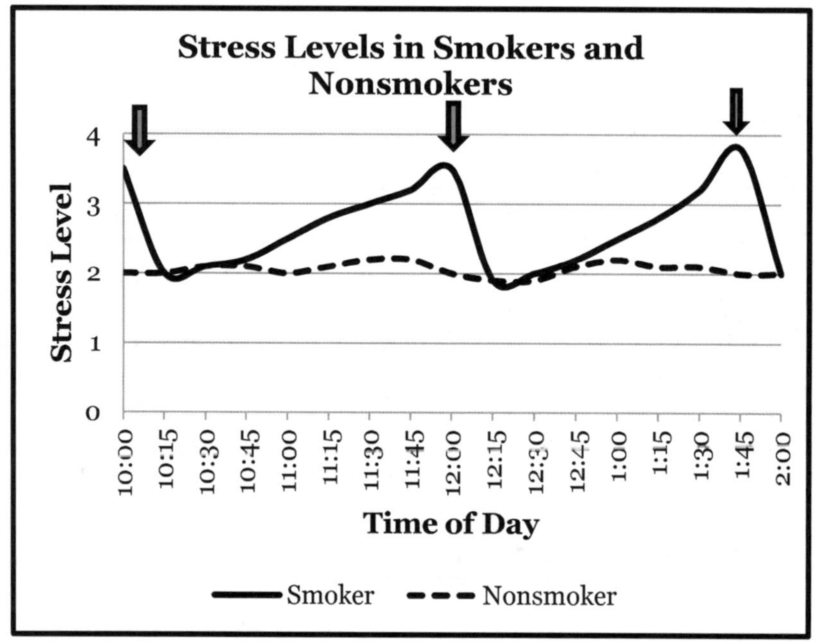

If smoking was really relaxing, smokers should be the most mellow, laid-back people. Nothing should upset them. In reality, when smokers, ex-smokers and nonsmokers are asked to keep track of how stressed they feel, smokers are much more stressed than either the ex-smokers or the nonsmokers. That is because nicotine withdrawal is making smokers feel stressed, sometimes over and over throughout the day. Once they get over the withdrawal, ex-smokers feel just as relaxed as nonsmokers. Smokers are not by nature more anxious people than nonsmokers, it is the nicotine withdrawal that makes them more anxious. Many smokers believe that they will not be able to cope with thc stress in their lives if they give up smoking, but ex-smokers report that their lives became less stressful after they quit smoking. We know that that is because they no longer experience withdrawal stress on top of the stress of daily living. Smoking wasn't relieving their stress, it was adding to it.

Much of the pleasure that people get from smoking seems to come from the relief of withdrawal symptoms. The more addicted people become to Nicotine, the more pleasure they get from smoking. If you take your fingernails and scratch your arm, it is unpleasant. But if you have an intense itch there, scratching in the exact same way feels so good. It relieves your discomfort. If you are like most smokers, your first exposure to Nicotine was unpleasant, but now smoking is pleasurable because it relieves your withdrawal symptoms. Most smokers say that the first cigarette of the day is the most pleasurable one, and that is probably because that is when their withdrawal symptoms are most intense because they have gone all night without smoking.

When you stop smoking, the nicotine withdrawal symptoms become more intense over the first few days but then they start to fade and most of them are gone within a week or two. Dr. DiFranza will tell you more about this in Book 2.

Chapter 8
Psychological Dependence

Before I go any further I want you to take the following test. You don't have to show your answers to anyone so be honest with yourself.

The Autonomy over Smoking Checklist	This statement describes me...			
	not at all	*a little*	*pretty well*	*very well*
When I go too long without a cigarette I get nervous or anxious.	1	2	3	4
When I go too long without a cigarette I lose my temper more easily.	1	2	3	4
When I go too long without a cigarette I get strong urges that are hard to get rid of.	1	2	3	4
When I go too long without a cigarette I get impatient.	1	2	3	4
I would go crazy if I couldn't smoke.	1	2	3	4
I rely on smoking to deal with stress.	1	2	3	4
I rely on smoking to take my mind off being bored.	1	2	3	4
I rely on smoking to focus my attention.	1	2	3	4
After eating I want a cigarette.	1	2	3	4
When I smell cigarette smoke I want a cigarette.	1	2	3	4
When I see other people smoking I want a cigarette.	1	2	3	4
When I feel stressed I want a cigarette.	1	2	3	4

Your answers to the first four questions tell you how much you suffer from nicotine withdrawal symptoms. We talked about those in the last chapter. You can add up your score for these four questions. The average adult smoker scores 6. Your score will tell you how bad your withdrawal symptoms are in comparison to other people.

The next four questions tell you how much psychological dependence you have on smoking. That is, how much you have convinced yourself that you need me to cope. Add up your score. The average adult smoker has a score of 5.

Now, I say "convinced yourself that you need me to cope" because I have never actually helped anyone cope. That's just not my thing. I am not your personal support system. Yet most smokers say they need me to cope with boredom and almost all smokers say they need me to cope with stress. I do appreciate all of this undeserved admiration, and it is so much sweeter because the irony is that I am the reason why you find it hard to cope with boredom and stress in the first place. I am not the solution to your coping problems, I am the cause. Get rid of me and you will cope better.

If you finished the 8th grade I am sure that you survived much boredom and many stressful situations. So how is it that you were capable of dealing with boredom and stress when you were 13 years old, but as an adult you need me to cope with boredom and stress? Let me explain how this happened to you.

Let's start with boredom. Normal people do not see boredom as something they need to cope with. When they have to wait and there is nothing to do, they relax and let their mind wander. They rest and day dream. Smokers are not so lucky.

If you remember, early withdrawal symptoms like Wanting can be ignored. If a smoker is busy, he or she may not even notice Wanting. If they notice Wanting, they can usually make it go away by busying themselves with something. Sometimes we get so busy that we don't notice that we are getting hungry. If we are occupied with something important our brains ignore things that are not important. When things quiet down, that is when you notice how hungry you are all of a sudden.

The same is true of Nicotine withdrawal. If you are really busy, you might not notice Wanting and Craving, but when you have nothing to do, you become aware of your Nicotine withdrawal symptoms. So it isn't that you need to smoke to cope with boredom. It is that whenever you have nothing to do, your mind focuses on your withdrawal symptoms. Nonsmokers and ex-smokers can relax when they have nothing to do, but smokers start to feel anxious and restless when they have nothing to do because the brain is focused on their withdrawal symptoms.

Now let's talk about stress. At least since the first time you stood up in front of the class to give a report, or had to get a filling at the dentist, you have had to deal with stress without freaking out. You developed ways to calm yourself down, stay in control and get through it. But somewhere along the way you may have developed the conviction that you need to smoke to deal with any stressful situation.

Nicotine Withdrawal Symptoms	**Stress Symptoms**
Anxiety	Anxiety
Restlessness	Restlessness
Irritability	Irritability
Difficulty concentrating	Difficulty concentrating
Difficulty sleeping	Difficulty sleeping

When smokers first experience Nicotine withdrawal, they may mistake it for stress. They try the methods that have always worked for them in the past when they were stressed, but these methods have no effect on the stress-like symptoms of Nicotine withdrawal. Then they smoke a cigarette, and like magic, all of their stress-like symptoms disappear in an instant. Over many years you may have relieved the stress-like symptoms of Nicotine withdrawal tens of thousands of times by smoking, and you have learned that smoking is the only way to cope with these symptoms.

It is only natural that when you feel real stress, your automatic reaction will be to reach for a cigarette. The problem is that I take away the stress-like symptoms of Nicotine withdrawal, but Nicotine has little effect on real stress symptoms. If you are a typical smoker, the first thing you do when you are stressed out is to smoke a cigarette. This is such an ingrained response that you don't even think about it. After smoking a cigarette you still feel stressed, so you smoke another, and another. If you watch a stressed-out smoker smoke, they don't suddenly heave a sigh of relief and chill-out, they look like a stressed-out smoker smoking, and they feel like a stressed-out smoker.

So even though you have a strong desire to smoke whenever you feel stressed, I am doing nothing to help you cope with the stress. You are on your own. You are still just as capable of dealing with real stress as you were when you were 13.

Being a smoker does not help you cope with stress, it makes it harder. When you are a smoker you might be in a situation where you are experiencing real stress plus the stress-like symptoms of Nicotine withdrawal at the same time, like a double whammy. That certainly doesn't help you cope. Ex-smokers never have to deal with the double whammy.

Chapter 9
Social Smokers

Back in the day when smokers were actually welcome in polite society some people called themselves "social smokers." They smoked only when they were socializing. Some of these people might smoke only two or three cigarettes per day and they would do that for decades and never feel the need to smoke more than that. It was said that these people were not addicted to nicotine. Perhaps they had a genetic mutation that made them immune to my powers of addiction. We may never know. Now that smoking in polite company is about as welcome as a case of herpes, pretty much anyone who is not addicted to Nicotine has already quit smoking.

What I have found is that in rare smokers, the Latency to Craving only shrinks so far, maybe down to two or three days and never gets any shorter. These people are comfortable as long as they smoke every few days. It really pisses me off that these people go around bragging that they are not addicted to me when they are. They think that just because they can go two or three days without smoking, it proves that they are not addicted. They are addicted, they just have a long Latency to Craving. Most of these folks have tried to quit many times unsuccessfully. If they weren't addicted they wouldn't be smoking.

Then I have to love those college students who think they are too smart to get addicted to me. They may smoke one or two cigarettes a day and they convince themselves that they aren't addicted because they never feel a Craving or a Need to smoke. They don't feel a Craving or a Need because they never stop smoking long enough. If they smoke one cigarette every night they won't feel Craving until their Latency to Craving shortens to less than 24 hours. I may have them hooked for a few years before that happens.

Here's a little secret for you. It can be just as hard to quit smoking when you are smoking a few cigarettes per week as when you are smoking a pack per day. If you are at the same stage of addiction, it doesn't matter how much or how little you smoke, you are going to go through the same thing when you try to quit. I know that nondaily smokers fail at their attempts to quit at exactly the same rate as daily smokers. So when these smart ass college students finally figure out that they are addicted while smoking only one cigarette per day, they are just as likely to fail when they try to quit as anyone else.

If you believe you are one of these social smokers with super powers that prevent you from getting addicted, here are two tests for you. The fastest way to tell if you are addicted is to go through the Hooked on Nicotine Checklist.

The Hooked On Nicotine Checklist	YES	NO
Have you ever tried to quit, but couldn't?		
Do you smoke now because it is really hard to quit?		
Have you ever felt like you were addicted to tobacco?		
Do you ever have strong cravings to smoke?		
Have you ever felt like you really needed a cigarette?		
Is it hard to keep from smoking in places where you are not supposed to, like school?		
When you tried to stop smoking...(or, when you haven't used tobacco for a while...)		
did you find it hard to concentrate because you couldn't smoke?		
did you feel more irritable because you couldn't smoke?		
did you feel a strong need or urge to smoke?		
did you feel nervous, restless or anxious because you couldn't smoke?		

If you say yes to any of these questions, you are hooked for sure. If you said no to all 10 questions you are not off the hook yet. Stop smoking for one month. Because the Latencies can be as long as a month, or maybe more, you have to stop smoking for at least a month to see if you experience Wanting, Craving or Needing.

I have heard lots of people brag that they never Need me, but when I challenge them to stop smoking for a few days, they can't. They had reached the Needing stage of addiction but didn't know it because they never stopped smoking long enough to feel it.

Chapter 10
What Happens When You Quit?

So far I have only told you how it is that you got from smoking your first cigarette to where you are now. If you are like most smokers, you wish you had never started smoking because you have tried many times to quit without success. I am going to describe what most smokers experience when they try to quit cold turkey. I am sure a lot of this will sound familiar.

The stage of addiction you are in determines what you experience when you quit. By now you have probably figured out which stage of addiction you are in. The table gives a brief summary of what smokers in different stages experience when they go too long without smoking.

Stages of addiction
No Addiction You can stop using tobacco for weeks at a time and it doesn't bother you. You have no withdrawal symptoms when you stop smoking.
Stage 1-Wanting Whenever you go too long without smoking you notice a mild desire to smoke that will go away in a short time if you ignore it. It isn't hard to ignore.
Stage 2-Craving Whenever you go too long without smoking the desire for a cigarette becomes so strong that it interrupts your thoughts and is hard to ignore.
Stage 3-Needing Whenever you go too long without smoking you feel an urgent need to smoke. The desire to smoke is so urgent that it is hard to concentrate on anything else. You feel that you won't be able to feel and function right until you smoke again.

The Wanting Phase

Whatever stage of addiction you are in, the first phase of Nicotine withdrawal is Wanting. Depending on your Latency to Wanting, the first desire to smoke may come a few minutes after you smoked your last cigarette, or a few weeks after you smoked your last cigarette. Since Wanting is mild, brief and easily ignored, you should have no difficulty dealing with it.

The Craving Phase

If you are in the Craving or Needing stage of addiction, you will next experience the Craving phase of Nicotine withdrawal. The Craving phase is more intense than the Wanting phase. Craving may interrupt your thoughts. In other words, you are concentrating on something, and then out of the blue, it seems like your brain is telling you it wants you to smoke. It isn't your imagination that your brain is telling you to smoke, your brain actually is telling you it is time to smoke. Without Nicotine, parts of your brain are getting out of balance. Your brain knows that I will put it back in balance and it is making you Crave a cigarette.

If you ignore the Craving, you can make it go away for a while, but it will be back. Throughout the day the Craving comes and goes. During the Craving phase you may also experience other symptoms of Nicotine withdrawal. You might start to feel a little anxious, like something isn't quite right. You might feel nervous or restless, like you have too much energy and don't know what to do with yourself. It is like your brain is on alert. It may be more difficult for you to get to sleep because of this.

If you are trying to quit smoking for good, you may remind yourself of all of the reasons why you want to quit.

Meanwhile, your brain is trying to talk you out of quitting. It may feel like you have an angel on one shoulder reminding you of all of the noble reasons why you should quit, while the devil, played by your brain, is on your other shoulder trying to talk you out of it. If you are in the Craving stage of addiction, this may be as bad as it gets.

The Needing Phase

If you are in the Needing stage of addiction, you will go through the Wanting phase of withdrawal, then the Craving phase of withdrawal and on into the Needing phase. Depending on your Latency to Needing, it may take you a few days to get to Needing, or it might take 15 minutes.

Needing to smoke is a much more intense and urgent desire to smoke than Craving. When you get to Needing, your brain misses me so much that is beginning to panic. It tells you that you need to smoke right now, and it won't let you concentrate on anything else. It is hard to concentrate on your reasons for wanting to quit while your brain is telling you that quitting is a huge mistake.

Any restlessness, nervousness or anxiety you felt during the Craving phase could become more intense during the Needing phase. You become impatient and irritable. You have a short fuse. You snap at people and get into arguments over nothing. If you have kids, you may start yelling at them over things that you would normally ignore. At this point, your loved ones may join your brain in telling you that quitting is a bad idea.

In addition to all of these mental symptoms, you may begin to experience physical symptoms of Nicotine withdrawal. Your hands may shake. You might develop a headache. You could experience discomfort in your chest, like you are not getting enough air, or you could get a discomfort in the pit of your stomach like you would if you were really hungry. Your mouth might go dry, or it might fill with saliva as if you could already taste your next cigarette.

Smokers in the Needing stage of addiction do not wait until they feel Needing to smoke. They smoke when they experience Wanting or Craving. Because of this, they think that when they quit, the worst thing they will experience is Craving. The first time they actually experience Needing is when they try to quit. Then they don't know what hit them.

Nobody could live with the Needing phase of withdrawal forever. Fortunately, if you can hold out long enough your brain figures out that it isn't going to get any more Nicotine and it starts to remodel itself so that it can regain balance without Nicotine. Your brain is like a bratty toddler that wants something. It throws a tantrum and makes a fuss, but if you don't give in, it will eventually give up and quiet down.

For the Rest of my Life

You would think that smokers would know all about Nicotine withdrawal, but I never met one who did. Nicotine withdrawal is like having the flu. When you have the flu, you feel miserable for the first two or three days, then you gradually feel a little better each day. Within a week or two you are back to normal. For most people, Nicotine withdrawal is like that. You feel miserable for two or three days and then little by little you start to feel better. Within a week or two you are back to normal, only better. Quitting smoking leaves you better off than when you were smoking, both physically and mentally.

Some smokers say that the worst Craving is on the first day after they quit and then it gradually gets better over the following weeks. However, most smokers say that the Craving actually gets stronger over the first three days after they quit. So for a few days the Craving becomes more intense and comes more frequently. In either case, over time, the Craving gets weaker and comes less and less often. After a few weeks, most ex-smokers experience Craving only once a day. With time, the Craving becomes just a Wanting which is easily ignored.

Unless they have successfully quit smoking in the past, smokers have no idea that all of the symptoms of Nicotine withdrawal are only temporary. When Nicotine withdrawal makes you impatient and irritable, you might assume that this is your true personality emerging. You might think "I'm a bitch" or "I'm a bastard" and if I don't smoke I will be a bitch or a bastard for the rest of my life. You might convince yourself that you are doing the world a favor by smoking.

Actually, the way you feel shortly after you smoke a cigarette is your natural mood and personality. That is how you will feel as an ex-smoker. It is Nicotine withdrawal that temporarily turns you into a bitch or a bastard. If you can stick it out, the normal you will return in a few days.

Like I said, smokers don't know anything about withdrawal. When they are having intense Cravings, they have no idea how long these will continue. They don't know whether they will experience these 20 times a day for the rest of their life, or for only a day or two. They think they are going to be miserable bastards for the rest of their lives if they don't smoke. They give up because they don't know there is a light at the end of the tunnel.

If you can stick with it, the worst of the withdrawal symptoms are gone within a week, although the Craving may occur every once in a while for years. Without the stress of Nicotine withdrawal throughout the day, ex-smokers say they are less stressed than when they smoked. Within a few days, irritation in the lungs clears up and you may notice that you get less winded when you exert yourself. Your sense of taste and sense of smell gradually come back. So, if you can suffer through Nicotine withdrawal, you will actually be and feel better off than you did when you were smoking.

Failure is not an option

With quitting cold turkey, failure is not an option, it is the rule. Failure is the expected outcome when you quit cold turkey. About 95% of smokers fail when they try to quit cold turkey. That is because I change your brain. I change the chemicals in your brain. I change the receptors on your nerves. I change how your nerves are connected to each other. I change how your nerves function together. Nicotine addiction is a biological disease. You would not expect to be able to cure other diseases like high blood pressure or heart disease with pure willpower. What gives you the idea that Nicotine addiction can be cured with willpower? Willpower can't change the chemistry of your brain anymore than it can make you into an Einstein, just because you would like to be smarter. Willpower cannot put your brain back in balance. So 95 times out of 100, smokers fail when they try to conquer this disease with willpower alone.

Some people have a Latency to Needing of only a few minutes. Such people may be overwhelmed with Needing within an hour of quitting smoking. Other people may not get to the Needing phase of withdrawal until several days after they quit. About half of would be quitters have already returned to smoking within 3 days.

Smokers find the Needing phase to be overwhelming, and after a struggle, they give in and smoke a cigarette. Within minutes, your suffering is over and your brain is happy, but you feel like a failure. You feel that you are too weak to quit smoking. You feel that if you had more willpower you would be able to quit. Everyone knows someone else who has quit smoking cold turkey. So when you fail, you feel inferior to all of the ex-smokers you know. You feel like you have a character flaw that prevents you from being successful at quitting.

When you try to quit and fail, it can be quite a blow to your self-esteem. You may have told everyone you know that you were going to quit smoking and now everyone will know that you failed. It can be humiliating. It may take you several years before you get up the courage and self confidence to put yourself through this again. Not only do you understand how unpleasant it can be to quit smoking, you also understand what a blow it is to your ego if you fail. Some people develop such a fear of failing that they are afraid to give it another try.

If willpower was all it took to quit smoking, you would have quit a long time ago. It isn't you. It's me. It isn't that you are too weak. I am a powerful drug that has permanently changed the chemistry of your brain. I have given you a brain disease. I have convinced your brain that it can't live without me. You have no control over these chemical changes in your brain. I have directed your behavior from your first cigarettes until now. I determined when you would smoke in the bathroom in school. I determined when you bought your first pack of cigarettes. I determine how long you can remain comfortable without smoking, and how many cigarettes you must smoke every day. And when you try to quit, I determine how you feel. The wanting, craving and needing. The short-temper, restlessness and trouble sleeping. I am in control of your brain, and your brain is in control of you. So that puts me in control of you. So yes, I get a little pissy when you blame yourself when you fail to quit. Like I had nothing to do with it? It's not you, it's me, and until you learn how to fight fire with fire, I am in control.

N

Book 2
Quitting Smart
by
Joseph R DiFranza MD

Chapter 1
What's Wrong With You?

Hi. My name is Joseph DiFranza and I have been practicing medicine as a family doctor for 30 years. After publishing more than 100 articles on smoking for scientists and doctors, it occurred to me that someone should write a book about smoking for smokers. This idea came to me when I realized that none of my patients who smoke had a clue about the nature of their addiction to nicotine. When they try to quit they don't know what they are doing. They are trying to accomplish something that is very difficult under the best of circumstances, but they are doing that while they are completely in the dark about what it is they are going through. Since they don't know what they are up against, they can't come up with a rational plan on how they are going to deal with it. In Book 1 Nicotine provided you with a guided tour of how it got you addicted and how that addiction controls your behavior. In Book 2 I will provide you with a guided tour of how you are going to conquer that addiction and take back control of your life.

The first thing I want to address is the argument that smokers can't quit because they lack willpower. This is an argument that the tobacco companies make so they can blame smokers for their predicament. Unfortunately, most smokers need no convincing that they lack willpower. When they fail in their attempts to quit smoking, they blame their failure on their lack of willpower. This is because they don't understand nicotine addiction.

To me, willpower is the ability to resist temptation. If smoking was just a simple pleasure, like eating dessert, willpower would be all it would take to stop smoking. But smoking is not just a simple pleasure, it is an addiction. I have had patients tell me that they hate smoking, but they can't stop. Smoking holds no temptation for them, but they Need to smoke. Nicotine addiction is not about pleasure, temptation and willpower.

Nicotine addiction is a neurological (nerve) disorder that is caused by exposing the brain to nicotine. Repeated exposures to nicotine cause chemical alterations in the brain. As a result, the brain needs nicotine to function normally. When your brain requires nicotine to function normally. It doesn't matter whether you like smoking, or how strong your willpower is, your brain needs nicotine to function normally.

So, if it isn't about willpower, why can some people stop smoking easily, while others can't? No two brains are identical. I know from my own research at the University of Massachusetts Medical School that people differ widely in how their brains react to nicotine. When I give nicotine to people in our MRI scanner, different parts of the brain become activated in different people. Because nicotine addiction is a biological disorder, the symptoms can vary greatly from one person to the next, depending on our genes. For many diseases, there are mild cases and severe cases. The same is true for nicotine addiction.

For some people, the symptoms of nicotine addiction are very mild. These people may brag about how easy it was for them to stop after smoking for 30 years. It <u>was</u> easy for them to stop because their symptoms were mild, not because they have more willpower than you do. For other people, the symptoms of nicotine addiction are quite severe, and they may find it impossible to quit on their own no matter how much determination and willpower they have.

One reason why smokers get down on themselves is that they know people who have quit smoking and they ask themselves, if that person can quit why can't I? The reason is not that you are weak and lack willpower; the reason is that your biology is different. Your addiction to nicotine may be much stronger than those of the ex-smokers you know. What you experience when you stop may be more severe than what they experienced when they stopped. So stop beating yourself up and let's get to work.

Chapter 2
What's Not Wrong With You?

What's wrong with you is that you have a biological addiction to nicotine. You might call it a physical or chemical problem with your brain. Your brain requires nicotine to function properly. Before we go on, I think it would be helpful to make it clear what nicotine addiction is not.

As we discussed in the last chapter, nicotine addiction is not caused by a lack of willpower. Nor is nicotine addiction caused by having a weak character. It is not caused by a personality flaw that causes you to place pleasure above all else. Nicotine addiction is not a result of an addictive personality. It is not a Freudian oral fixation. It is not just a bad habit. And, I am going to go stick my neck out here and declare that nicotine addiction is not a "mental disorder."

The term mental disorder implies some disturbance in thinking, mood or behavior. For over 30 years, the American Psychiatric Association has classified nicotine addiction as a mental disorder. But now that we know more about how the brain works, I think it is time that we define it as a neurological (nerve) disorder.

Some authorities define nicotine addiction as a "maladaptive behavior." Certainly, smoking is maladaptive in relation to maintaining good health, but as Nicotine explained, smokers' behaviors are a logical adaptation to their brains' need for nicotine to function properly. Just as diabetics must supply themselves with insulin to function normally, smokers must supply themselves with nicotine to function normally. Their behavior is not irrational; it is required by a chemical problem in the brain.

The primary symptom of nicotine addiction is the hunger for nicotine which smokers experience as Wanting, Craving and Needing. Yes, the hunger for nicotine is a mental experience, but that does not make nicotine addiction a mental illness. Pain is also a mental experience. Many medical conditions, like headaches and menstrual cramps, have pain as their only symptom, but we don't call them mental illnesses. Although the symptoms of nicotine addiction are mostly mental experiences, nicotine addiction is a neurological problem. Since neurological problems are considered medical problems and not psychiatric problems, in my book, being addicted to nicotine does not mean that you are mentally ill.

Smokers would probably prefer not to be labeled as mentally ill, but I think this distinction between mental illness and biological illness is important for another reason. When nicotine addiction is defined as a neurological illness, smoking becomes a symptom of that illness. If you want to get rid of the symptom (smoking), doctors should treat the brain to cure the addiction. If you cure the brain, people would not need to smoke. The stop smoking medicines that are currently available are the first efforts to fix the brain chemistry so that people can stop smoking.

Mental Illness View	Biological Illness View
Smoking is the problem.	Smoking is a symptom.
	Messed up brain chemistry is the problem.

The approach is entirely different when one considers smoking to be a mental illness. When authorities call smoking a maladaptive behavior, smoking is not a symptom of a deeper problem, smoking *is* the problem. Therefore, treatment is aimed at the behavior. Stop smoking and the problem is gone.

Even the most skilled therapists do not know the words to say to fix the chemistry of the brain. Success rates for smoking cessation counseling are poor no matter where you go, and despite the hundreds of millions of dollars spent each year on research, success rates for counseling have not improved one bit over the past 50 years.

The most important consequence of whether nicotine addiction is viewed as a mental illness or a neurological disorder is what happens when the patient can not quit.

Mental Illness View	Biological Illness View
Smoking is the problem	Smoking is a symptom.
The smoker has learned a bad behavior.	Messed up brain chemistry is the problem.
When treatment does not work, the blame falls on the smoker for continuing the behavior.	When treatment does not work, it is a failure of treatment.

Under the view that smoking is a mental illness, when the patient continues to smoke after receiving a talking therapy, the responsibility for the failure falls on the patient who did not change his or her behavior. Under the biological (neurological) view, if the patient continues to smoke, the responsibility falls on the medicine which failed to control the addiction.

As an analogy, let's consider patients who can't stop scratching. The mental illness view would consider scratching to be a maladaptive behavior. Treatment would be aimed at convincing the patients to stop scratching. They would be given advice on how to change their behavior. If the patients continue to scratch, it is their own fault that they are not getting better. Perhaps this is because they are mentally ill, illogical, self-destructive, uncooperative, weak-willed, or stubborn.

Under the medical view, the behavior of scratching would be seen as a symptom of a deeper problem. The doctor would ask the patients why they are scratching. They would answer of course, that they are itchy (which by the way, is purely a mental experience). The doctor would then prescribe medicine to take away the itch. If the patient is still scratching the following day, both the doctor and the patient would conclude that the medicine failed to do its job. Nobody would blame the patient.

So which view do smokers believe applies to them? Based on my experience I would say that 100% of smokers believe in the mental illness view. When the treatment does not work and they cannot stop smoking, smokers always blame themselves. They attribute the fact that they could not stop smoking to their lack of willpower and weak character. They are embarrassed and tend to avoid the doctor. This is exactly the opposite of how patients behave when they feel that their symptom is from a medical problem.

If my prescription for itchiness does not work, my patients do not blame themselves for scratching. They call me the next day wanting a "stronger" medicine. If my prescription does not cure insomnia, my patients want a stronger medicine. If my prescription doesn't take the headache away, I hear about it. Menstrual cramps, heart burn, constipation, whatever it is, if I don't fix it the first time, my patients will be back. This is the medical view of illness, if the patient is not getting better, it is not because they are weak willed; it is because the therapy is not working.

On the other hand, if a patient desperately wants to quit smoking and my prescription doesn't work, I won't hear a word. They don't call. They don't write. They don't mention it at their next physical. That is because they are ashamed. Although the medicine failed to cure their addiction, they put the fault on themselves. I have never had a patient come back and say, "That stop-smoking medicine you gave me two weeks ago didn't work, I want something better." If patients thought of smoking as a medical problem, they would come back until they were better, but they don't. When the medication doesn't work, they feel embarrassed and ashamed. They feel like a failure. Many smokers feel so bad about themselves when they are unable to stop that they are actually afraid to try again.

What's NOT wrong with you? You are NOT mentally ill because you smoke. You have a medical problem, not a problem of character or willpower. Relapsing back to smoking when you are trying to quit is a key symptom of addiction. Relapse is caused by the chemical imbalance in your brain. It is a symptom of your medical condition. Relapse indicates that the treatment was not successful; it is not something that you should be ashamed of. A relapse is no reason to avoid your doctor. It's just the opposite. As soon as you relapse, you should hold your head high and make another appointment.

I have heard smokers say that they thought that smoking was too trivial a problem to be bothering their doctor about. As a medical problem, nicotine addiction has a mortality rate of 50%. In other words, half of smokers die from a disease caused by smoking. This makes smoking of more concern to doctors than the headaches, itchy rashes, menstrual cramps, heart burn, insomnia and constipation that fill our days. If you have decided it is time for you to quit, you should be in your doctor's office every week until you are cured, or until your doctor tells you he or she has nothing left to offer you.

Chapter 3
Nicotine Withdrawal

Quitting smoking may be the hardest thing you ever accomplish. If you are taking the time to read this book, chances are that you have tried to quit and failed many times. Quitting smoking is much scarier than it has to be because smokers do not understand their addiction at all. Smokers do not understand what is going on in their brain when they quit. They do not know if their suffering will ever end.

Knowing how nicotine actually changes your brain chemistry, you may wonder how it is even possible for anyone to quit smoking. Since the brain comes to need nicotine to stay in balance, how do ex-smokers do it? Why do they not crave nicotine every minute for the rest of their lives? The answer is that the brain will not allow itself to remain out of balance for long.

If you can deprive your brain of nicotine for long enough, it will adapt to life without nicotine. When you stop smoking, your brain immediately begins to adapt to the absence of nicotine. Eventually, it reaches a point where it no longer requires nicotine to remain in balance. At this point you will be a happy ex-smoker.

So how long does it take for your brain to get to the point where it no longer needs nicotine to function normally? Nobody knows exactly, but we do know that it varies from one person to the next. Some people feel like they are back to normal a few days after they have quit smoking, and most feel normal a few weeks after they quit. Doctors call the time between when you stop smoking and when you feel normal again, the withdrawal period. Although your brain may immediately set to work to rid itself of its need for nicotine to function normally, this takes time. In the meantime, you are going to experience nicotine withdrawal.

When smokers fail at their attempts to quit, it is almost always during the withdrawal period. Getting through the withdrawal period is what quitting smoking is all about. Yet, I am always amazed that my patients know next to nothing about nicotine withdrawal. They do not know how long withdrawal symptoms last, and they do not know how to cope with them. Nicotine withdrawal is the reason quitting smoking is so hard. So you have to understand what it is all about.

When you first stop smoking, things start to go a little haywire in your brain. Let us assume you have reached the Needing stage of addiction. When you stop smoking, you will go through the Wanting stage of withdrawal, the Craving stage of withdrawal, and then the Needing stage of withdrawal.

In the Wanting stage you will experience the mild desire to smoke that you can ignore. If you hold out, you will advance to the Craving stage next. Craving is a stronger desire to smoke that is hard to ignore. It feels like your brain is telling you to smoke, because it is. Your brain is out of balance without nicotine and it is trying to get you to smoke. Depending on your Latency to Craving you may reach the Craving stage of withdrawal a few days after you stop smoking, or you may reach it a few minutes after you stop smoking. Most people say that the Craving comes and goes, that they may have an intense craving for a few minutes, but then it goes away and comes back later.

If you manage to get through the Craving stage without smoking, things go from bad to worse. In the Needing stage of withdrawal your brain will not let you think of anything other than how much you would like to smoke. Your brain may be getting panicky and make you feel that something bad is going to happen to you if you do not smoke.

Wanting, Craving and Needing come from an imbalance in one part of your brain, but this is not the only part of your brain that is messed up. While you are going through the Wanting, Craving and Needing stages of withdrawal, other parts of your brain begin to malfunction without nicotine to keep them in balance. There are parts of your brain that are in charge of making you feel irritated or angry. It is normal to feel irritated or angry under the right circumstances. As these parts of your brain get out of balance without nicotine, they become hyperactive. You start to feel irritated for no good reason. You get angry for no good reason. As other parts of your brain start to get out of balance without nicotine, you start to feel restless or fidgety for no reason. You start to feel nervous or anxious for no reason. You may have trouble sleeping for no reason. Without nicotine, all of these parts of your brain start to go haywire. As they do, you may start to feel out of control. You are trying to stay calm and cool and yet that is not how you are behaving. You cannot concentrate on your work. You start snapping at people. You are not crazy, so you do realize that the way you are feeling and behaving is not appropriate.

I have had patients tell me that as they were experiencing these symptoms, they did not know that they were withdrawal symptoms; they thought that this was their true personality emerging. They thought that smoking was the only thing that allowed them to pass as a normal person, and if they did not start to smoke again, they would be a nervous wreck for the rest of their lives. I have had patients tell me that they got so nasty when they were in withdrawal, that the same loved ones who begged them to quit smoking asked them to start again. Obviously, people do not realize that these personality changes are withdrawal symptoms and that withdrawal symptoms are always temporary.

Shortly after you quit smoking, your brain is already adapting to life without nicotine. Usually within two or three days the irritability, anger, nervousness, restlessness and anxiety begin to fade away as your brain gets back into balance without nicotine. Your normal personality will come back. The worst part of withdrawal usually lasts only a few days.

With time, Needing fades back into Craving, and Craving fades back into Wanting. People are very different from one another in how long Needing, Craving and Wanting stay around. Some smokers say they just quit smoking and never had a desire to smoke again. These mutants were never addicted in the first place. I call them mutants because they probably have some favorable genetic mutation in their nerves that protected them from developing an addiction to nicotine. For normal people, the worst craving is during the first few days after quitting. It comes and goes. It may last only a few minutes and then come back an hour later. Sometimes the cravings are weak and other times they are strong. Nobody knows why.

When you are in withdrawal, your brain is telling you that it is out of balance without nicotine. Your brain is trying to convince you that you want to smoke because your brain actually believes that nicotine is what it needs to function properly. In a way your brain is right. It does need nicotine to function properly. But what your brain doesn't know is that it can learn to function properly without nicotine. Your brain functioned just fine without nicotine from the time you were born until you started to smoke. If you deprive your brain of nicotine for long enough, it will change so that it can once again function properly without nicotine. Given enough time, your brain will heal itself. Your job is to deprive your brain of nicotine long enough that it can heal itself.

Chapter 4
Cold Turkey vs Medication

The term "cold turkey" refers to the goose flesh that heroin addicts experience when they go through withdrawal from heroin. Their skin gets cold and clammy and the hairs stand on end. Someone must have thought that they resemble a cold plucked turkey. When you stop smoking cold turkey it means you suffer through nicotine withdrawal without medication.

The good news is that your brain will heal itself if you can make it through the withdrawal period without smoking. The bad news is that out of every 100 smokers who are trying to quit "cold turkey," 95 won't make it through the withdrawal period. That is not because 95 out of every 100 people lack willpower. It is because withdrawal is too much for most people to handle.

Before modern times, quitting cold turkey was a smoker's only option. About half of all the living people who ever smoked in the United States have quit smoking, and 95% of them did it cold turkey. So how is it that 95% of people fail to quit when they do it cold turkey, and yet almost half of all smokers have quit by going cold turkey?

The answer to this paradox is that they have to try over and over and over and over until they are successful. If each time you try to quit cold turkey you have a 5% chance of success, by the time you have made your tenth attempt, you are up to a 50% chance of success. If you try to quit every year, it may take you only 10 years to reach the point of having a 50% chance of success. But persistence is no guarantee of success. I have patients who have failed at cold turkey 30 times.

If your withdrawal symptoms are too severe, you may never be able to quit smoking without medication, medication that will gradually wean you off nicotine, or relieve the imbalance in your brain. Medication can increase your chance of success with each attempt to quit from the 5% for cold turkey, to 10%, 20% or 30% depending upon which medication you use. That doesn't guarantee you success on your first attempt, but it greatly reduces the number of attempts it should take you to quit.

It is funny that smokers will never give up on cold turkey no matter how many times it has failed for them, but they only give a medication one chance to work. If the medication doesn't work the very first time, they never try it again. They go back to cold turkey.

For many years, doctors were frustrated because they had nothing to offer people who were addicted to nicotine. There were no effective medications. Through decades of research, scientists have developed three types of medications that improve a smoker's chances of success with quitting. Now, doctors are frustrated because so many smokers are reluctant to take the medications that were developed to help them. Let's look at some of the reasons why this is the case.

One reason is that some smokers feel that the fact that they have not been able to quit shows that they are weak and lack willpower. By now I would hope that I have convinced you that your inability to stop smoking has very little to do with willpower. Nicotine addiction is a chemical imbalance in your brain; it is not a lack of willpower. But once smokers have convinced themselves that they lack willpower, they believe they need to stop on their own without medication to prove to themselves that they can do it. It becomes a matter of pride. Because they suffer from the delusion that they lack willpower, quitting smoking cold turkey becomes a test of their character. Because they feel they have something to prove, using medicine to stop smoking feels like cheating. If they quit smoking with the medication they might see that as proof that they didn't have the willpower to stop on their own. It becomes more important to them to prove that they have willpower than it is to achieve their goal of stopping smoking.

This is sad but funny at the same time. As a family doctor, I treat patients with all kinds of diseases. Other than nicotine addiction, I can't think of a single disease that people feel that they have to refuse medication out of pride. When I tell patients that they have pneumonia and need to take an antibiotic, they never give me an argument. They don't tell me that they need to battle the pneumonia on their own without help to prove to themselves that they are strong enough to do it. Common colds are caused by viruses, and these particular viruses are immune to every antibiotic we have. Antibiotics are useless against the common cold, and prescribing antibiotics for colds is not only a waste of money, but it leads to antibiotic resistance in bacteria, which is a big problem. When you take an antibiotic for a cold it will do you no good, and you could have side effects. You could develop an allergy to the antibiotic, or you could spread antibiotic resistant bacteria to your loved ones. Yet some of the same people who demand an antibiotic prescription from their doctor every time they have a common cold will refuse to take medication to help them quit smoking. Obviously, they do not feel that taking medicine for a cold is cheating or copping out. Only when it comes to nicotine addiction does pride interfere with people taking their medicine.

Another reason people give for not wanting to take medicine is that they don't like the idea of putting a substance in their body. One day a young man in his late 20's came in to see me for a routine physical exam. As this was the first time I had met him, we spent the first part of the visit reviewing his past medical history. He had had no serious illnesses and was on no medications. When I asked him about substance use he seemed to take pride in listing all of the illegal street drugs he had used. It seems his experimentation with illegal drugs had been quite thorough as it didn't seem that he had missed any. We then proceeded to the physical exam and I noted that his blood pressure was dangerously high. As he got dressed, I explained that his high blood pressure put him at risk for a variety of potentially fatal problems, and that it was so high that I recommended that he start on medication immediately. He refused the prescription and said that he didn't like the idea of putting chemicals in his body.

I am telling this story because many smokers tell me that they don't want to take a nicotine replacement product to help them stop smoking because they are concerned about the safety of these products. They are more concerned about taking prescription medication than they are about continuing to smoke. I am going to talk about medication safety issues later, but here I just want to comment on the idea that the prescription nicotine products might be more dangerous than cigarettes.

The nicotine in the gum, patches, sprays and lozenges that are sold by pharmaceutical companies to help people stop smoking is chemically pure. It is not contaminated with any other chemicals. These products are manufactured in spotless, sterile facilities under government inspection. They are subject to strict quality standards in terms of the purity of the nicotine and the dose. All of these products have been tested for safety and effectiveness in dozens of studies with smokers. All of them deliver less nicotine than you would get from smoking. As far as we know, nicotine does not cause any diseases. All of the diseases caused by smoking are caused by the other chemicals that are in the tobacco.

The nicotine that you get from an all natural cigarette, made from organically grown tobacco without any additives, comes along with over 4000 other chemicals in the smoke. These “all natural” chemicals include radioactive elements and chemicals that are used in antifreeze, cleaning products, and embalming fluid. Dozens of these chemicals are known to cause cancer. The manufacturers also add hundreds of other chemicals to their cigarettes. The identity of these secret ingredients has never been revealed to the public. The manufacturing facilities do not have to pass government inspection and of course there are no safety tests that cigarettes have to pass. The safety of tobacco smoke has been thoroughly tested over the past 400 years by human volunteers like you, and we know that this mixture of chemicals kills half of the people who smoke. If you consider your body to be a temple, in my opinion, it would be much better to pollute it with one safe chemical (nicotine) than 4,000 dangerous chemicals.

Many of my patients have told me that they don’t like the idea of taking a medicine to help them stop smoking because they are concerned about whether it is safe to take a prescription medicine. All prescription drugs must be tested for safety before they can be approved for use. Out of the thousands of drugs approved for sale, every year a few are removed from the market because it is discovered that they have a harmful side effect that was not detected in the safety studies. Drug safety studies usually involve hundreds of volunteers, but once a drug is approved for sale it may be taken by millions of patients. Very rare side effects do not show up in a study that includes only a few hundred people, but would show up when millions of people start to take the drug. When a drug is removed from the market because of safety concerns, it may be for a side effect that affects only one patient in 10,000. All of the drugs prescribed to help smokers quit have been used for many years by millions of smokers and there no documented safety problems with any of these medications. If there is some unknown dangerous side effect it would have to be very rare or it would have been discovered by now.

Now it is important to balance the risk of taking these medications against the risk of not taking the medication. Maybe there is a very rare side effect that doctors don't know about yet. Let's imagine an unlikely scenario in which it is discovered that stop smoking drugs killed 1 out of every 10,000 people who took them? Would you take a stop smoking drug if it gave you a 1 in 10,000 chance of dying?

You need to weigh the risks of taking the drug against the risk of not taking the drug. The risk of not taking the drug is that you will continue to smoke. Out of 10,000 smokers who are unable to stop smoking, 5,000 die from smoking (I'm not making this up). So if you take the drug, you have an imaginary risk of 1 in 10,000 that the drug will kill you, and if you don't take the drug and continue to smoke, you have a real risk of 5,000 out of 10,000 that smoking will kill you. In other words, in the worse-case scenario where doctors discover that quit smoking drugs actually kill 1 in 10,000 users, you are still 5,000 times more likely to die from smoking than from taking the medicine. Any person concerned about their personal safety should demand the medicine.

Another argument I often hear about the nicotine replacement medications is that my patients don't want to substitute one addiction for another. The purpose of the nicotine replacement products is to wean you off nicotine, not to keep you addicted for the rest of your life. But even if you were to use a nicotine replacement product for the rest of your life, it wouldn't hurt you, and it would save you money. I will talk more about this later.

I wanted to address all of these common concerns up front, so that you will not harbor misconceptions about the relative safety of medical treatment as compared to continuing to smoke, and so that you will not refuse help out of pride generated by the misconception that nicotine addiction, unlike any other disease, is a test of your character.

Chapter 5
Know Your Enemy

No two brains are exactly alike, and it may be that no two people face exactly the same thing when they try to stop smoking. In this chapter you are going to size up your own addiction to nicotine so you can prepare a battle plan for dealing with it.

Let's start with the Hooked on Nicotine Checklist. To determine how strong your addiction to nicotine is, answer the following 10 questions.

The Hooked On Nicotine Checklist	YES	NO
Have you ever tried to quit, but couldn't?		
Do you smoke now because it is really hard to quit?		
Have you ever felt like you were addicted to tobacco?		
Do you ever have strong cravings to smoke?		
Have you ever felt like you really needed a cigarette?		
Is it hard to keep from smoking in places where you are not supposed to, like school?		
When you tried to stop smoking...(or, when you haven't used tobacco for a while...)		
did you find it hard to concentrate because you couldn't smoke?		
did you feel more irritable because you couldn't smoke?		
did you feel a strong need or urge to smoke?		
did you feel nervous, restless or anxious because you couldn't smoke?		

Now count the number of questions you answered 'yes' to. That is your HONC score. When I have given the Hooked on Nicotine Checklist to adult smokers, people have had scores ranging from zero to 10. If you answered no to all 10 items, you are probably not addicted to nicotine. If you answered yes to any of these items, you are addicted.

As you can see from the graph, smokers cover the whole range of HONC scores from zero to 10. The average HONC score is 7. But keep in mind that these scores represent only the smokers who are still smoking. The average for smokers who have quit would be lower, because the lower your HONC score, the better chance you have of quitting.

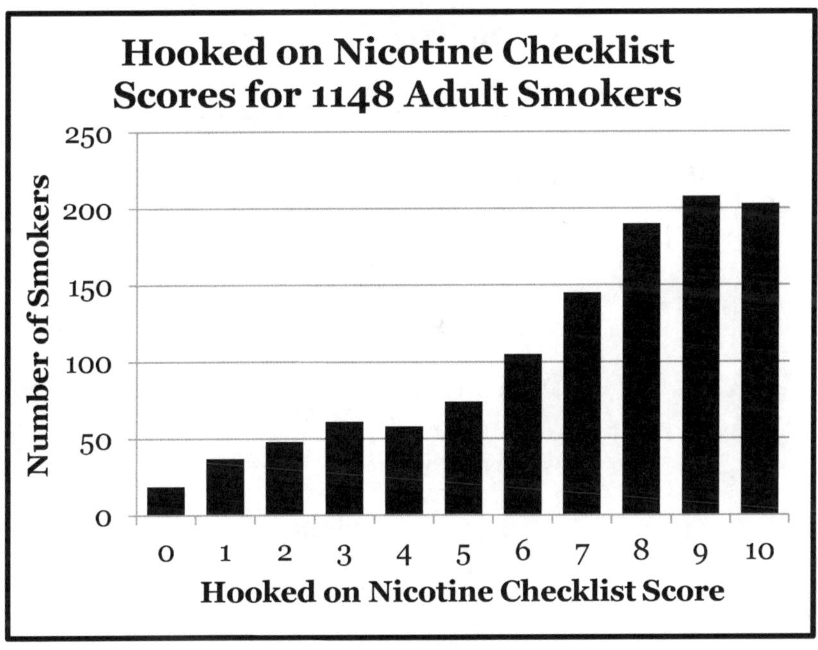

What I hope you get out of this exercise is that smokers differ greatly in the severity of their addiction to nicotine, from none at all, to severe. The higher your HONC score, the more likely you are going to need medical treatment to stop smoking. So if you have a HONC score of 10, you should not be comparing yourself to the person with a HONC score of 2 who is bragging about how easy it was to quit.

There are three things that make it hard for smokers to stop: withdrawal symptoms, cues that make you want to smoke and psychological dependence on smoking.

Withdrawal symptoms

We have already discussed withdrawal symptoms so I have only a few things to add. You will remember that after your brain gets adapted to nicotine, it doesn't function right without nicotine. Different people experience different withdrawal symptoms when they stop smoking. The table lists the most common symptoms of nicotine withdrawal. You may have a withdrawal symptom that it is not listed here. The way you can tell it is a withdrawal symptom is that it comes on whenever you stop smoking, and it goes away immediately if you smoke a cigarette or two.

Nicotine Withdrawal Symptoms
Type A symptoms
Wanting, Craving, Needing
Type B symptoms
Anxiety
Bad mood
Difficulty concentrating
Dry mouth
Empty feeling in the stomach
Headache
Increased appetite
Irritability
Muscular tension
Restlessness
Short temper
Tight feeling in the chest
Tremors
Trouble sleeping

In the table I have called Wanting, Craving and Needing **Type A** withdrawal symptoms because these are the symptoms that make it hard to quit. The **Type B** withdrawal symptoms may be annoying and unpleasant, but they are not the ones that are telling you to smoke. If you only experienced type B symptoms, quitting would be pretty easy.

Typically, these symptoms are not too severe and are gone within a few days.

The type A withdrawal symptoms are purely there to get you to smoke. In the first book, Nicotine talked about how your brain gets you to do things for it. When it needs energy, it makes you hungry so you will eat. When it needs water, it makes your mouth dry and makes you thirsty so you will drink. When it wants you to breathe, it gives you the sensation that there is not enough air in your chest so you will breathe. It shouldn't be surprising then that when the brain wants nicotine, some people say it feels like they have hunger pains in their belly. Others say it feels like they are thirsty and their mouth gets dry. Other people say it feels like there is not enough air in their lungs.

When physical sensations like these do not succeed in getting you to smoke, your brain takes it to the next level. It starts to play mind games with you. It starts to put ideas in your head.

If you are trying to stop smoking, it is because you have decided that is what you want to do. You may have a lot of good reasons for quitting. Your brain works at convincing you that you don't really want to stop. It helps you think up lots of reasons why you should keep on smoking. It tries to discourage you, to convince you that you can't do it. It tells you that resistance is futile, you might as well give up now and spare yourself the agony. Or, it will tell you that just one cigarette won't hurt. It tricks you into thinking that smoking one cigarette will actually help you to quit smoking by "taking the edge off." So quitting smoking is like having an angel on one shoulder and a devil on the other, giving you advice. Only in this case, your brain is the tricky devil trying to tempt you into doing something that is bad for you.

The following test will let you compare your withdrawal symptoms to those of other smokers.

This describes me...	*not at all*	*a little*	*pretty well*	*very well*
When I go too long without a cigarette I get nervous or anxious	0	1	2	3
When I go too long without a cigarette I lose my temper more easily	0	1	2	3
When I go too long without a cigarette I get strong urges that are hard to get rid of	0	1	2	3
When I go too long without a cigarette I get impatient	0	1	2	3

For each question you have four choices that are scored from zero to 3. Add up your answers to get your withdrawal score. The graph on the next page shows Withdrawal scores for 346 adult smokers so you can see how you compare. The numbers on the left side of the graph indicate the number of smokers, and those across the bottom of the graph indicate the different scores from 0-12. The average score for an adult smoker is 6. The higher your score, the more likely you will benefit from a stop smoking medication to take the edge off.

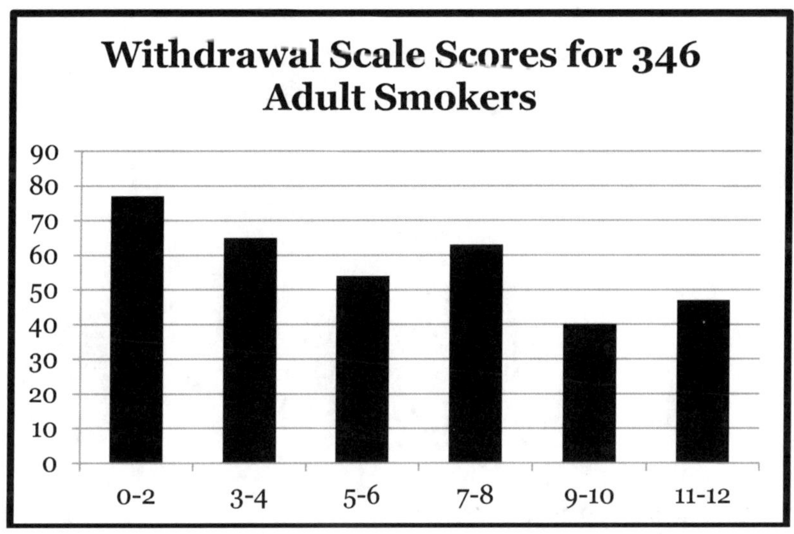

Sensory Cues

Withdrawal is the biggest cause of craving when you are quitting smoking, but most smokers know that there are certain cues that can cause them to crave a cigarette. The next test will help you see if you are more or less responsive to these cues than other smokers.

This describes me…	*not at all*	*a little*	*pretty well*	*very well*
After eating I want a cigarette	0	1	2	3
When I smell cigarette smoke I want a cigarette	0	1	2	3
When I see other people smoking I want a cigarette	0	1	2	3
When I feel stressed I want a cigarette	0	1	2	3

Add up you score. The next graph shows the Cue scores for 346 adult smokers. The average score for an adult smoker is 7.

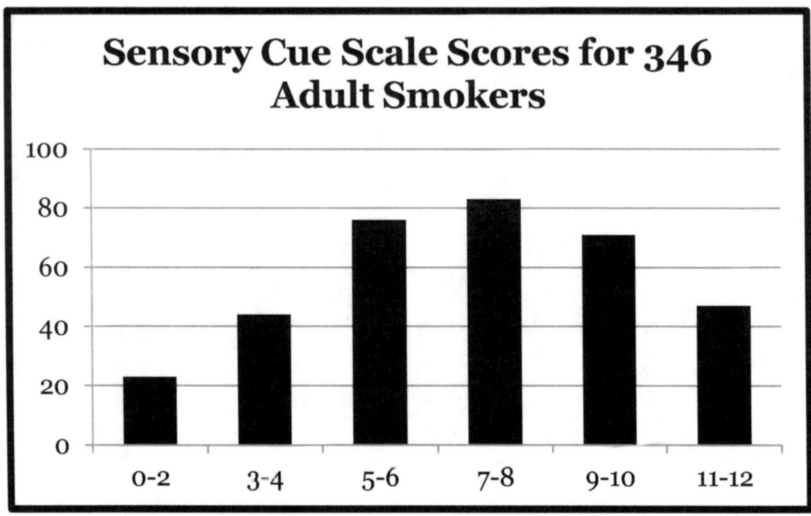

This test lists only a few common cues that might make you crave a cigarette. Some situations make you crave a cigarette because they stimulate your senses the same way as smoking a cigarette. For as long as you have been smoking, your brain has linked the sight and smell of cigarette smoke with the jolt of nicotine it got with every cigarette. If you smoked 20 cigarettes per day for 20 years that would be 146,000 doses of nicotine. Each time you smoke you pair the sights and smells with a little blast of nicotine to your brain. When you see a cigarette or smell the smoke, your brain anticipates the nicotine and it may make you crave a cigarette. Craving a cigarette because of these sensory reminders of smoking is usually not as strong as the craving you get from withdrawal. However, being around other people who are smoking when you are trying to quit can make it harder on you because of this craving.

Nobody knows how long these sensory reminders of smoking continue to provoke craving after you quit. Several ex-smokers have told me that even decades after they stopped smoking, the smell of cigarette smoke still gives them a little craving to smoke. Other ex-smokers have told me that they now hate the smell of cigarette smoke. They can't stand being around someone who is smoking. You should hope that you end up like these people because they are unlikely to go back to smoking.

Over your lifetime you have developed habits and routines around smoking. You tend to smoke at certain times of the day, or when you are doing certain things. You might smoke whenever you are in your car, or whenever you are talking on the phone. Most smokers enjoy a cigarette after each meal. Smoking at particular times or events is not part of the addiction, but you might find yourself automatically reaching for a cigarette when you are in one of these situations.

Breaking these habits may be the easiest part of quitting smoking. Everybody has certain routines built into their day from the moment we get up. Do you take your shower before you eat breakfast or after? Do you brush your teeth before you take a shower or after? You may have followed the same routine all your life, but if it would add 8 years to your life if you did these things in a different order, you would have no trouble changing your routine.

Psychological Dependence

Nicotine had you take this test on psychological dependence, but it would be helpful for you to do it again.

Describes me...	*not at all*	*a little*	*pretty well*	*very well*
I would go crazy if I couldn't smoke	0	1	2	3
I rely on smoking to deal with stress	0	1	2	3
I rely on smoking to take my mind off being bored	0	1	2	3
I rely on smoking to focus my attention	0	1	2	3

These questions determine if you have a psychological dependence on cigarettes. The graph on the next page shows psychological dependence scores for 346 smokers. The average score is 5.

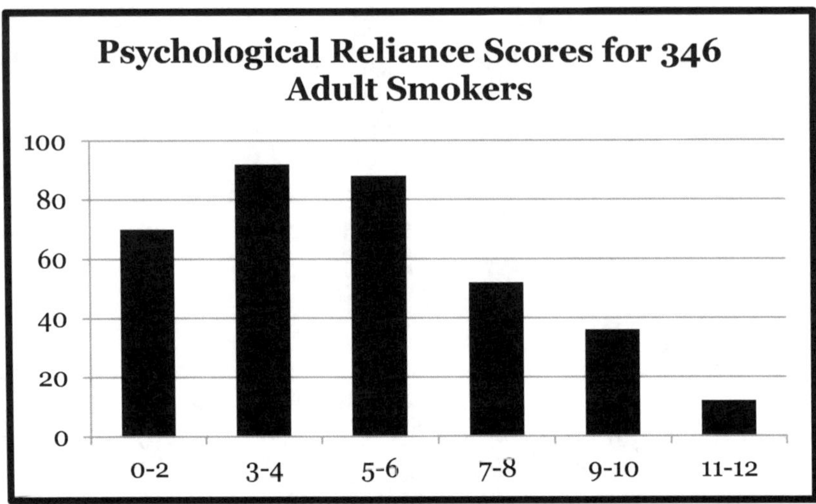

When you have a psychological dependence on smoking, it means that you believe in your mind that you rely on smoking to help you cope. The most common form of psychological dependence is relying on smoking to cope with stress. Nicotine already explained that much of the stress that smokers experience is due to withdrawal from nicotine. So stress does increase during nicotine withdrawal, but once you get through withdrawal, your stress levels will be less than when you were smoking.

The graph on the next page shows an experiment in which scientists measured muscle tension in smokers and nonsmokers. When the smokers were in withdrawal, their muscles were more tense than the muscles of nonsmokers. The arrows in the graph indicate when the smokers smoked a cigarette. When the smokers smoked their muscle tension was reduced to the point where it was the same as that of the nonsmokers. This study showed that smoking is relaxing, if you are in nicotine withdrawal.

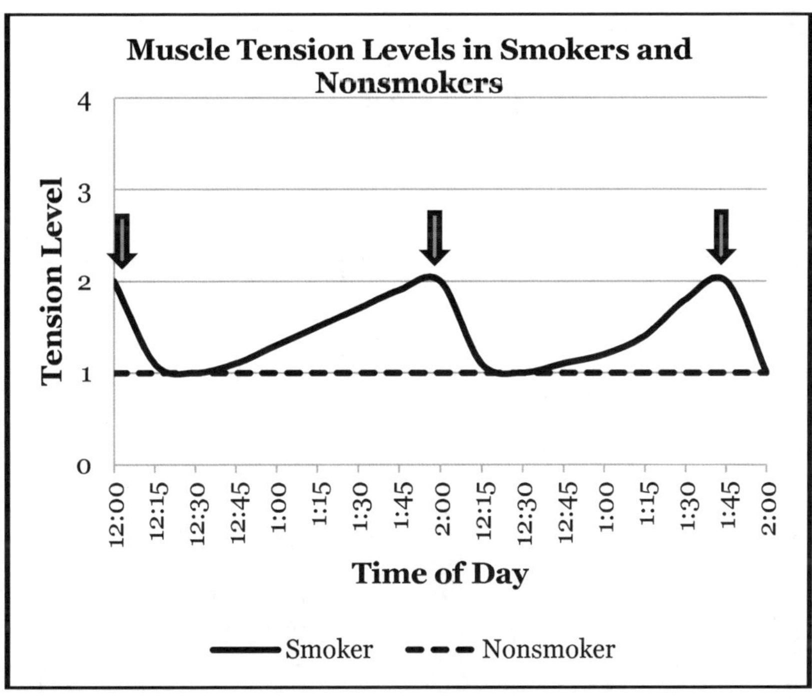

When anxiety, irritability and restlessness are caused by nicotine withdrawal, they go away within minutes of smoking a cigarette. Nicotine helps you relax when withdrawal is making you uptight, but when you are in a stressful situation, it actually does very little to calm you down. If it did, stressed out people would be all calmed down after smoking one cigarette. But they aren't, so they smoke another and another. If your first reaction to any bad news is "I need a cigarette," then you are psychologically dependent on tobacco and that is going to be something you will have to overcome if you want to stop smoking.

Your Overall Addiction Score

The Hooked on Nicotine Checklist gave you a score telling you how addicted you are. If you add up your scores to the three tests you just completed it will give you an idea of how hard it will be for you to quit in comparison to the average smoker. Add up your scores for Withdrawal, Cue-induced Craving, and Psychological Dependence. The possible range of scores is from zero to 36. The average overall score for an adult smoker is 18. If your score is below average, that does not mean that quitting will be easy. Since 95% of all smokers don't make it when they go cold turkey, only smokers with very low scores would find it easy to quit on their own.

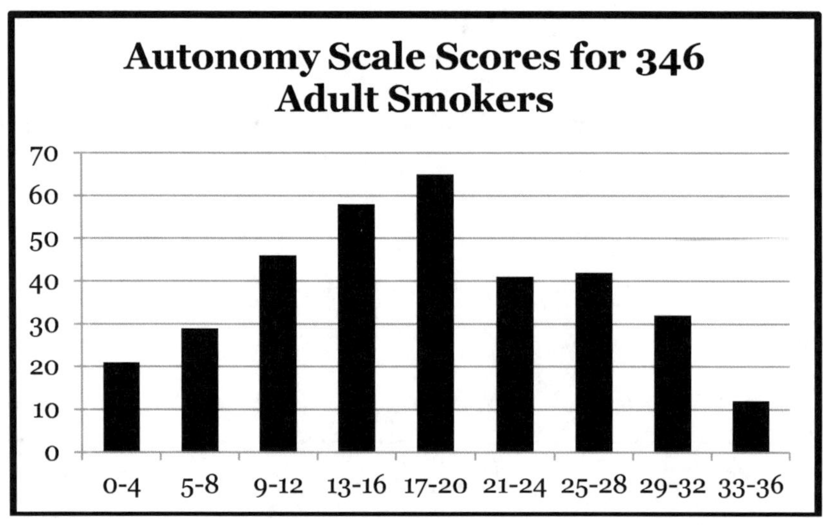

Now that you have identified the things that stand in your way, the next chapter will help you design a game plan for dealing with these obstacles.

Chapter 6
Your Game Plan

Before the big game, a coach will study the opposing team. He or she will try to discover their strengths and weaknesses and use that information to design a game plan to defeat them. But the opposing coach is doing the same thing.

In the first book, Nicotine taught you the rules of the game. Now you understand your addiction to nicotine. You know that your brain now needs nicotine to stay in balance. You understand what nicotine withdrawal is, what its symptoms are, and how long it lasts. You understand what psychological dependence on cigarettes is, and how your senses of sight and smell can trigger craving when you are with someone who is smoking. Now it is time to use your knowledge to come up with a game plan to defeat your addiction to nicotine.

As you work to defeat your nicotine addiction, your opponent is your brain, and who knows you better than your brain? Your brain thinks it cannot survive without nicotine. It is going to hit you with its best game every time.

Your brain has three power players, Withdrawal, Psychological Dependence, and Sensory Cues. The tests you took in the last chapter give you the stats for how these three play against your team. Take a second and write in your scores from those three tests. If your Withdrawal score is high, that means that Withdrawal scores a lot of points against you.

Withdrawal	Psychological Dependence	Sensory Cues

We are going to discuss strategies for dealing with each of these three power players, but remember that the winning point could be scored by the weakest player on the opposing team, so it is important that you have a game plan that deals with all three. This is your book, so take out a highlighter and highlight every strategy that you think might be helpful to you. You don't want to put all your eggs in one basket. You want to use as many strategies as you can.

Your brain has one major vulnerability; its offense gets weaker over time. If you deprive your brain of nicotine it will desperately do whatever it can to get you to smoke a cigarette, but at the same time it is already making the necessary adjustments so that it can be in balance without nicotine. As your brain gets used to doing without nicotine, its offense gets weaker and weaker, and eventually it gives up. All you need to do to win is stay in the game. If you can refrain from smoking a single cigarette, you win. Withdrawal, Psychological Dependence and Sensory Cues will be history. However, if you give in and smoke one cigarette, it could restore your opponent to full strength.

Here is how it works. As you struggle to keep from smoking, your brain is making the necessary adjustments so that it can be in balance without nicotine. These adjustments are your secret weapon. They weaken your opponent every day. As these adjustments come into play the type B withdrawal symptoms get weaker and weaker. The cravings get weaker. If you can hold out, these adjustments will eliminate your opponent. However, smoking one cigarette destroys the adjustments and returns your opponent to full strength. This could be three days after you stopped smoking, or three year. One cigarette is all it takes to restore your addiction back to its original strength.

Say you had two teams of smokers competing for which team could rack up the most days without smoking. Everyone quits smoking on the same day. After two days nobody has smoked, but everyone is experiencing craving. One team decides that it wouldn't really be cheating if their team all smoked two cigarettes just to "take the edge off," and that is just what they do. At this point, which team would you bet on?

A scientist did this experiment. He found smokers who were willing to stop smoking for 2 weeks. After all of the subjects in the experiment had stopped smoking for 2 days, he allowed half of them smoke 2 cigarettes. He then asked all of the subjects how much craving they were experiencing. As you might expect, the subjects who had just smoked reported less craving. But the next day their craving came back with a vengeance. Those 2 cigarettes wiped out all of their progress and they were back to square one. The subjects who had not been allowed to smoke were more likely to make it through the 2 weeks without smoking. The subjects who were told to smoke 2 cigarettes relapsed back to smoking much sooner. The moral of the story is that smoking a cigarette when you are trying to quit is like throwing the game. It erases all of the points you had scored and restores your opponent to full strength.

Defending Against Withdrawal

Your brain's first attack will come from Withdrawal. You know how long you can go without a cigarette before you experience Craving or Needing. That is how much time you will have before you will have to start dealing with withdrawal symptoms. Here are some strategies. You don't want to give your opponent any easy points. You should use every strategy that applies to your situation.

Attack #1 Type B Withdrawal Symptoms

Type B withdrawal symptoms make you feel crappy. You are feeling restless and nervous. You can't concentrate. You have a headache. You can't sleep. You are very irritable and have a short temper.

Defensive Strategies

The first thing is to recognize this attack. Before you knew about nicotine withdrawal, you might have thought that some of these symptoms were just your normal personality emerging. These symptoms are not you; they are the symptoms of nicotine withdrawal. When you have the flu and you get a headache, fever and muscle aches, you don't think "this is me." You think "this is the flu." When you are experiencing the symptoms of nicotine withdrawal, especially the mental symptoms, it is important to think "this is not me, this is nicotine withdrawal."

This is important because some smokers give up on quitting because they think that the withdrawal symptoms they experience are the real them. If you get irritable or short tempered, tell yourself that these mood and personality changes are just withdrawal symptoms. This is not your normal personality coming out. It is just that certain parts of your brain are temporarily out of balance as your brain gets used to life without nicotine. Your normal personality and mood will return in just a few days.

If you know that nicotine withdrawal makes you unfit for human company, you may want to arrange to be alone for a few days and hole up somewhere with a pile of books you never have the time to read, or rent a pile of movies. Call in sick. If you had the flu, nobody would think there was a problem if you called in sick for a few days. When insurance covered it, alcoholics were given 4 to 6 weeks out of work for inpatient treatment. As a doctor, I would have no problem with excusing a patient from work for a few days to cure their addiction to nicotine. Because they are more prone to respiratory infections, smokers are absent from work more often than nonsmokers. Taking a few days off to quit smoking will cut down on future sick days, saving your employer money in the long run, not to mention the reduced cost of providing health insurance for ex-smokers as compared to smokers.

Knowing that withdrawal symptoms are temporary will help you weather the storm. Keep in mind that you are not going to feel this way for the rest of your life. Most smokers say that type B withdrawal symptoms last only a few days, and they are almost always gone after a week. Keep saying to yourself that this is like the flu; if you suffer through it for a few days everything will return to normal. If you have experienced withdrawal in the past, you have a good idea of what symptoms you can expect. Be prepared.

If nicotine withdrawal gives you a headache, take a few Tylenol. If nicotine withdrawal gives you trouble sleeping, don't be afraid to take an over-the-counter sleeping pill for a few days. This is a perfectly appropriate use for these medications. You don't want to be facing nicotine withdrawal tomorrow on half a night's sleep. You need to be on top of your game. If you are healthy, you could take 50 to 75 milligrams of Benadryl. This is not habit forming, and it doesn't interact with stop smoking medications.

Some smokers deal with the restlessness they get from withdrawal by starting to exercise. You could sign up for a gym membership or just walk around the block. If you have too much energy you might as well take advantage of it. I have had several patients who lost weight when they quit smoking because they started going to the gym.

All of the quit smoking medications are designed to take the edge off of withdrawal symptoms. For some people, the stop smoking medications provide great relief for these symptoms. If you are like most people, when you get the flu you take over-the-counter medicines to get relief from the symptoms. Popular flu remedies contain pain relievers, fever reducers, decongestants, antihistamines and cough suppressants. If you have no qualms about taking 5 different medications when you have the flu, you should not be afraid to take something to relieve the symptoms of nicotine withdrawal. Over-the-counter flu medicines will not save your life; a stop smoking medication could save your life if it makes it possible for you to make it through withdrawal without smoking.

Attack #2 Type A Withdrawal Symptoms

Wanting, Craving and Needing. In the last chapter we compared your brain to having a devil on your shoulder that is giving you a stream of bad advice. Remember that when you are trying to conquer your addiction to nicotine, your brain is working for the other team. Your brain is like a trash talking player trying to get under your skin so you will mess up. It keeps telling you that you can't do it.

Defensive Strategies

If you made it less than a week the last time you tried to stop smoking, then you were probably over powered by Craving of Needing. Most likely you will need some medication on your side to cut these opponents down to a size you can manage. First I want to talk about nonmedicinal strategies.

Craving does not remain at a constant level. It comes and goes and is stronger at some times than others. A craving can come on like a contraction in labor. It starts to build, reaches a peak and goes away. During childbirth, women are told to ride out one contraction at a time and rest in between contractions. In Lamaze classes women are taught how to focus on their breathing to distract them from the pain of the contractions. Ex-smokers who successfully dealt with their waves of craving say they did this by distracting themselves from the craving. The craving is your brain trying to talk you into smoking. There is no law that says you have to listen. Successful ex-smokers say that when they first sensed a craving coming on they would immediately distract themselves by doing something else. It is difficult to concentrate on two things at once, so by concentrating on something else, it is difficult to concentrate on the craving. The more you distract yourself from the craving, the faster it will go away.

All your brain wants is a few minutes alone with you, a few uninterrupted minutes. The last thing you want to do is give your brain time to work on you. You do not want to plan a long monotonous car trip for when you plan to quit. You do not want to sit there and dwell on the craving. Craving is worst when you have nothing to do, and is least troublesome when you are busy. Successful ex-smokers stayed busy when they were going through withdrawal. They planned their days so they would be busy from morning to night. This is a good defense strategy. Do not give your brain a chance to work on you and wear you down.

Another strategy is to mentally distance yourself from the craving. By this I mean that you need to constantly keep in mind that it is not you that is craving a cigarette. <u>You</u> do not want to smoke a cigarette. <u>You</u> want to stop smoking. It is your brain that wants the cigarette, not you. When you are thinking, “I really want a cigarette,” you should realize that it isn’t you talking, it is your brain tricking you. When you hear yourself thinking “I want a cigarette right now,” you should catch yourself and say, “my brain wants a cigarette and is trying to trick me into smoking."

If you are watching a really scary movie and your fear gets overwhelming, you can remind yourself "it's only a movie." This distances you from the scary situation and makes it possible for you to handle your fear. By identifying the source of the craving as your brain and not you, it has the same effect as saying "it's only a movie." When you visualize the craving as coming from a source other than you, it may make it easier to cope with. To do this, each time you experience craving you should remind yourself that it isn't you that really wants a cigarette, it's your brain.

It might help to visualize your craving as your worst enemy. Your worst enemy is trying to make you fail. Every time you get a craving you can use it as an opportunity to tell that jerk what he can do with his craving. There is no reason why you can't trash talk. Put that irritability and short temper to good use. While you are trying to figure out the best string of curse words to direct at your enemy, you have taken your mind off of the craving.

Alcohol may intensify nicotine withdrawal. Having a drink can bring on strong cravings for a cigarette. After a few drinks you become an easy target for nicotine's seduction. This is true even after you have stopped smoking for a long time. More long time ex-smokers relapse to smoking when they are partying than when they are stressed out. While it is not necessary to give up drinking forever in order to quit smoking, it is an excellent defense strategy to avoid alcohol until you are out of the woods with withdrawal.

In its attempts to trick you into smoking, your brain is going to be trash-talking you. It will tell you that you can't do it. It will tell you that you don't want to stop smoking. It will make you feel miserable and then tell you that stopping smoking isn't worth the misery you are going through. It will be giving you 100 reasons why it would be a mistake to stop smoking.

Most smokers are ambivalent about quitting. Part of them wants to stop smoking and part of them doesn't. On the one hand they see the expense and all of the health reasons, but on the other hand, they enjoy it or depend on it. When you decide to quit, it is because at that moment you see the arguments in favor of quitting as being more important. But once you are in the throws of withdrawal, all of those reasons for continuing to smoke look a lot better. The angel on your shoulder is reminding you of all the reasons for quitting while the devil on your other shoulder is telling you why you should smoke again. You don't want to be reconsidering your decision to stop smoking every day while you are feeling miserable and can't concentrate.

It is a good defense strategy to consider the pros and cons of quitting before you quit. Make two lists, the reasons why you want to quit, and the reasons why you want to smoke. Under the reasons for smoking you can put that quitting is much harder than you realized. Don't even try to quit smoking until you are convinced that the reasons for quitting definitely outweigh the reasons for smoking. Then keep that list with you and read it over whenever you begin to doubt that you have made the right decision.

Your brain's most effective argument is that you should smoke just one cigarette to take the edge off. It will say "one cigarette won't hurt you," or "one cigarette a day is a lot better than the pack a day you were smoking before you quit," or "your chances of quitting will be better if you smoke one cigarette now to get you through it." It seems so harmless to smoke just one cigarette, but your brain is trying to convince you to throw the game. Once you smoke that cigarette, it is over. The nicotine from that cigarette wipes out all the progress your brain has made in learning to live without the nicotine and it has to start over. If you think of withdrawal as a week long ordeal through the woods to get to the other side, smoking a cigarette puts you right back at the edge of the woods where you started.

If you are feeling like you need one cigarette to take the edge off, you should be on stop smoking medication to make the craving more manageable. If you are already on a stop smoking medication, you need an adjustment to your medication. I will talk about this in the next chapter.

Attack #3 Cues

Sensory cues and situational cues can trigger an urge to smoke. Situational cues are places or activities that you associate with smoking such as drinking alcohol, being in a bar, celebrating, socializing with friends, finishing a meal, talking on the phone, and driving. When you are in the habit of smoking in one of these situations your brain may have you automatically reaching for a cigarette, just like you may daydream on your way to work and automatically make all of the correct turns without thinking about it.

Defensive Strategies

A habit is not the same thing as an addiction. You are addicted to nicotine, but you are not addicted to smoking while you talk on the phone. This is just part of your routine. Still, when you are trying to quit smoking, it is helpful to avoid situations that are going to make you reach for a cigarette automatically.

Many ex-smokers tell me that when they were quitting they tried to avoid situations that they associated with smoking. If they smoked a cigarette with their coffee every morning, they switched to tea for a few weeks. If they usually went to the break room to have a smoke during their coffee breaks, they instead went outside for a walk and some fresh air during their breaks. If they would ordinarily sit at the table and have a smoke after a meal, instead they would get up from the table and go brush their teeth. If they always smoked in the car, they would instead keep a pack of gum in their car and chew gum while they drove. Some would distract themselves from smoking by taking a new route to and from work so they would have to concentrate on their driving. In other words, they shook up their routines so that smoking would not be missed.

Other people have told me that they broke their smoking habits before they stopped smoking. For instance, if they were in the habit of smoking while driving, they stopped doing that while they continued to smoke at other times. After meals, they stopped smoking at the table. They got used to talking on the phone without smoking. What they were doing was disrupting their smoking routines so that when they did quit, these habits would not make it more difficult. It also gave them time to establish new habits that did not include smoking for all of their common daily activities. This is a smart strategy because it breaks quitting down into two steps (1) break all of your smoking habits while you continue to smoke, (2) stop smoking and deal with withdrawal.

The stop smoking medicines are designed to take the edge off withdrawal, but they don't seem to do anything to block the effects of these cues. Unless you had a score of zero on the cue test, you should pick a strategy to defend against these situational cues.

Some smokers will remove all reminders of smoking from their house and car before they stop smoking. They hide or throw out their ashtrays. They use up any remaining cigarettes and hide their lighter. They clean out the ashtray in their car. They don't want to be exposed to these cues that might trigger a craving.

Many smokers say that their attempt to quit failed because they were with someone else who was smoking and the cigarette smelled too good. If this has happened to you, or if you checked off that the smell of a cigarette makes you want to smoke, then the only defense is to avoid situations where people will be smoking until you are sure that you are not going to be tempted.

Some of my patients who are ex-smokers told me that they had to stay out of bars and avoided being in the presence of friends who smoke until they were sure that they were not at risk for starting to smoke again. Other ex-smokers told me that they arranged to spend their free time in places where smoking is prohibited so they would not be tempted.

The real challenge is when your partner smokes, or everybody in your family smokes. When parents smoke, their kids are more likely to smoke, and *their* kids are more likely to smoke. So there are families where most of the adults and teenagers are smokers.

It can be difficult to quit smoking if your partner continues to smoke. About 80% of all smokers want to quit, so usually, both partners want to quit. It isn't a bad idea to quit together, but what often happens is one partner starts smoking again, and that triggers a relapse in the other partner because they are constantly with someone who is smoking. If your partner wants to quit with you, a reasonable agreement is that if one starts to smoke, they will respect the other by not smoking in their presence. You should also agree that after the quit date, nobody smokes in the house or car.

If your partner is not interested in quitting, not ready to quit, or unable to quit, they should still be willing to agree not to smoke in the house or car. The idea that a smoker would not smoke in their own house or car might seem unreasonable, but national surveys reveal that 70% of smokers live in smoke-free homes. Many smokers live with nonsmoking spouses, children, or parents who would be harmed by exposure to second hand smoke. Most smokers are considerate about exposing other people to a health hazard and do not smoke in their own homes. There are even smokers who can't stand the smell of cigarette smoke and just don't want their home to smell bad. So if smoking is currently permitted in your home and car, that should stop before you stop smoking. It will be very difficult for you to stop smoking while you are exposed to the smell of cigarette smoke in your home. Also, if you go through all the trouble of quitting, you do not want to expose yourself to many of the same health hazards by breathing second hand smoke. Spouses, relatives and friends should respect your need and desire for a smoke-free home. By making your home and car smoke-free zones before you quit smoking, you will get out of the habit of smoking in the places where you will be spending much of your time after you quit.

If your spouse is not ready to quit, the least they can do is to agree to a smoke-free home to support your effort to quit, and to protect your health after you succeed.

Because the craving that is triggered by the sight and smell of smoking is not driven by withdrawal it does not go away when the withdrawal period is over. That means that the smell of a cigarette could trigger a relapse long after you are out of the woods with nicotine withdrawal.

Attack #4 Psychological Dependence

Almost all smokers rely on smoking to deal with stress. In other words, almost all smokers believe that smoking helps them deal with stress. You are psychologically dependent on smoking when you believe that it would be hard for you to cope without smoking.

Defensive Strategies

As we discussed earlier, smoking does not cure stress. In survey after survey, smokers rate their stress levels higher than ex-smokers do. If smoking really helped people deal with stress, people should report that their lives become more stressful after they stop smoking, but they don't. After people stop smoking, their lives become less stressful because they are not in nicotine withdrawal throughout the day. They still have ordinary stress, but they don't get the double whammy of the stress of withdrawal on top of ordinary stress. If you stopped smoking, the way you handle stress now after you have a cigarette would be the way you would handle stress all the time. You wouldn't need a cigarette to help you cope with stress.

It might help to ask your friends and relatives who have stopped smoking how they now cope with stress without smoking. They might not understand your question, because they aren't doing anything differently. They are handling stress the same way they have handled it all their lives. They just have less stress to deal with now because they don't smoke.

Cigarettes do not magically make stressful situations disappear. Smoking does not prevent people from having a "nervous breakdown." Now, when you are stressed, you smoke some cigarettes. But after smoking you are still stressed, and so you deal with it. All the times you have dealt with stress since the day you started smoking, you did it on your own. The cigarettes didn't solve a single stressful situation for you.

Caffeine improves performance on many tasks, but nicotine, no. After hundreds of studies, scientists are still looking for proof that that nicotine improves performance on something. What they have found is that nicotine withdrawal degrades performance on just about anything you might ask a smoker to do, from memorizing a list of words to driving a car. Give smokers nicotine and they perform as well as nonsmokers, not better. It is not that nicotine helps you perform better, it is that nicotine withdrawal makes you perform worse.

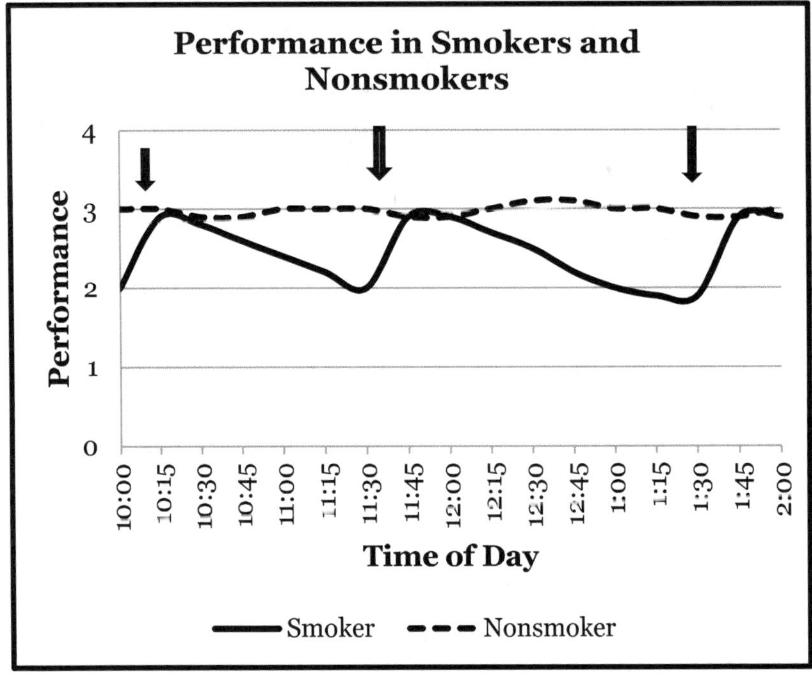

In the figure, the arrows indicate when the smokers smoked. Smoking restores performance to normal but withdrawal makes performance worse. So, in reality, smoking does not actually help people deal with life. That is just an illusion. But if you believe that you can't cope without a cigarette, it may be hard to commit yourself to quitting.

There has been no research on how people overcome the belief that they need to smoke to cope. I do know that when people stop smoking, after they have dealt with a few stressful situations without smoking, they gradually become convinced that they can cope without smoking. If you are so convinced that you need to smoke to cope with stress it might be helpful to handle a few stressful moments without smoking before you decide to quit. Convince yourself that you are a competent person who can handle a stressful situation without falling apart. If you work in a smokefree workplace, you have probably already handled many stressful situations without a cigarette.

Another possible strategy to convince yourself that you do not need cigarettes to cope might be hypnosis. Hypnosis is real and it does work to help people quit smoking. Hypnosis works on the power of suggestion. If you believe that you can't cope with life without smoking, you might ask a hypnotist to plant the idea in your head that you are a competent person who does not need to smoke to cope.

Psychological dependence is just a mind game that keeps you smoking. The way to fight a mind game is with another mind game. You know that your opponent, nicotine addiction, grows weaker every day that you don't smoke a cigarette. In your mind you should celebrate every single day without smoking as an additional point scored against your opponent. As long as you don't smoke a cigarette your opponent's score is zero. If you go three days without smoking the score is three to zero. Add another point to your lead every day you complete without smoking.

Another mind game is to remind yourself everyday that you have managed to cope without smoking without falling apart. Remind yourself that you handled every situation throughout the day without smoking. If you are a rational person, every day that you complete without smoking should add to your confidence that you can cope without cigarettes. Every day that you go without smoking should reduce your psychological dependence on cigarettes.

I hope you have identified lots of the strategies that might be helpful to you. The next chapter will discuss one strategy to avoid.

Chapter 7
Tapering: A Strategy to Avoid

Since withdrawal can be so unpleasant and difficult, why not avoid it altogether by gradually cutting down on how much you smoke each day until you have quit? Doctors call this tapering. Tapering is usually Plan B for smokers who have tried to quit cold turkey. It is a great idea that works with nicotine replacement products but doesn't work with cigarettes.

In the first book Nicotine told you about **Elective** cigarettes. Elective cigarettes are those that you smoke because you want to, not because you need to. **Required** cigarettes are those that you have to smoke because your Latency has run out and you are having craving.

I have asked smokers what percent of their cigarettes are Elective cigarettes and what percent are Required cigarettes. On average, smokers say that 50% of their cigarettes are Elective and 50% are Required. Smokers with a long Latency to Wanting have more time between Required cigarettes and they have a higher percentage of Elective cigarettes. Smokers with a very short Latency to Wanting smoke fewer Elective cigarettes.

Back when cigarettes were a lot cheaper, my patients would smoke on average one pack of cigarettes per day. When they were trying to quit by tapering they would gradually cut back to a half a pack per day. Then they would get stuck. They could never seem to get below a half pack per day. I used to think that there was something special about a half pack per day. That was before I discovered the Latencies.

When my patients were smoking a pack per day about half of their cigarettes were Elective cigarettes. When they began tapering down, they gradually eliminated their Elective cigarettes. When they got down to half a pack per day, all of their cigarettes were Required cigarettes. Their Latency would not allow them to space their cigarettes any farther apart. Willpower allowed them to eliminate all of their Elective cigarettes but none of their Required cigarettes. Elective cigarettes are smoked for pleasure. Required cigarettes are smoked to keep your brain in balance. Willpower will allow you to forego pleasure, but it will not keep your brain in balance. If you are not addicted to nicotine and all of your cigarettes are Elective cigarettes, willpower is all you need to quit. I have never met an addicted smoker who successfully quit by tapering.

If you want to quit by tapering, you should. But you should do it with a medicinal nicotine replacement product, not with cigarettes.

Chapter 8
Stop Smoking Medicines

If you can't get through the first two weeks of withdrawal without smoking, then you need medication to relieve your withdrawal symptoms. There are three medicines that are sold in the US that relieve both the Type A and Type B withdrawal symptoms. They differ in how effective they are at relieving these symptoms, but all have been proven to help people stop smoking.

These medications make the craving and needing more manageable, and relieve irritability and the other Type B withdrawal symptoms. Some people get nearly complete relief of withdrawal symptoms, while others say the medicine just takes the edge off. One medication may do nothing for you, while another could be very effective. The only way to know is to try each one until you find the one that works best for you. Let's discuss these medications one at a time.

Nicotine Replacement Treatment

Nicotine replacement treatment or NRT refers to nicotine products that are sold by drug companies to help you quit smoking. Nicotine products that are sold by tobacco companies to feed your addiction are not considered NRT.

NRT products are designed to help you taper yourself off of nicotine so that you don't experience withdrawal. Nobody understands why it is possible to wean yourself off of nicotine using these products but not with cigarettes.

The nicotine gum and patch have been available in the US without a prescription since 1996. These NRT products deliver pharmaceutically pure nicotine without the 4000 dangerous chemicals found in tobacco smoke. As far as we know, nicotine by itself does not cause any diseases, so you could use these medications for the rest of your life without endangering your health.

Most smokers do not get much benefit from NRT products because they do not use them correctly. Mistake #1 is not using enough to prevent withdrawal. When it comes to NRT, one size does not fit all. You have to figure out what is the right dose for you. Your doctor can't tell you and you can't go by what it says on the package. You have to figure this out for yourself.

One reason why people may need different amounts of NRT is that the intensity of their withdrawal symptoms differs. People in Stage 1 will not need as much relief from withdrawal symptoms as people in Stage 3.

A second reason why people may need different amounts of NRT is that their Latencies are different. The latency tells you how long one cigarette will keep withdrawal symptoms away. If a cigarette keeps your withdrawal symptoms away for only an hour, you will need to use NRT more often than someone who gets more lasting relief from a cigarette.

A third reason why people need different amounts of NRT is that they are used to getting different amounts of nicotine from smoking. People differ in how much nicotine they were using before they quit. Some people smoke more cigarettes than others. Some cigarette brands deliver more nicotine than others. Even so, if two people each smoked one cigarette of the same brand, one could get twice as much nicotine as the other. One person may smoke further down the cigarette, or inhale more deeply, or hold the smoke in their lungs longer, or smoke the cigarette faster so the nicotine level reaches a higher peak in the blood. In general, the more you smoke or dip, the more NRT you will need to prevent withdrawal.

A fourth reason why people might require different amounts of NRT is that they differ in how quickly their body eliminates nicotine. If your body eliminates nicotine faster, you will need to use more of it.

A fifth reason why people need to use different amounts of NRT is that the dose of nicotine you get from NRT products differs from person to person. The amount of nicotine you get from the patch may vary depending on how thick your skin is, and how much blood is flowing through it. Another factor is how well the patch sticks to your skin. The amount of nicotine you get from the nicotine gum will depend on how quickly you chew it, how often you swallow, or what you have just had to drink.

For all of these reasons, you have to find the right dose of NRT for your needs. The right dose of NRT is the dose that prevents you from feeling any withdrawal symptoms when you first stop smoking. If you are feeling withdrawal symptoms you are not using enough NRT. No matter how much NRT you are using, it isn't enough. It might seem like you are using a lot, but obviously your brain is not getting nearly as much nicotine as it did when you were smoking. If your brain is telling you that it wants a cigarette, you are obviously not using enough NRT.

Smokers want to be free from their dependence on nicotine as soon as possible. But the purpose of switching from cigarettes to NRT is not to immediately cut down on nicotine. Your goal with NRT is not to eliminate nicotine from your body as quickly as possible. The faster you do that, the worse your withdrawal symptoms will be.

Your first goal with NRT is to switch your brain from the sharp peaks and valleys of nicotine that you get from cigarettes to a constant level of nicotine that is high enough to prevent withdrawal. Given enough time, your brain can adjust itself to any level of nicotine, from none to very high. But it can't do both at the same time. For your brain to adjust, it needs a specific target that isn't moving rapidly up and down every time you smoke a cigarette. Tapering with cigarettes probably does not work because nicotine levels go from one extreme to the other. With NRT, nicotine is delivered much more slowly and over a longer period of time, so the fluctuations in nicotine levels are much smaller. This gives your brain a target to shoot at. Once your brain gets adjusted to a constant level of nicotine, you slowly move the target down to zero. This means that over 3 months or more, you gradually reduce the amount of NRT you use so that your brain has plenty of time to make constant adjustments that allow it to remain in balance with less and less nicotine, until finally, it is in balance without nicotine.

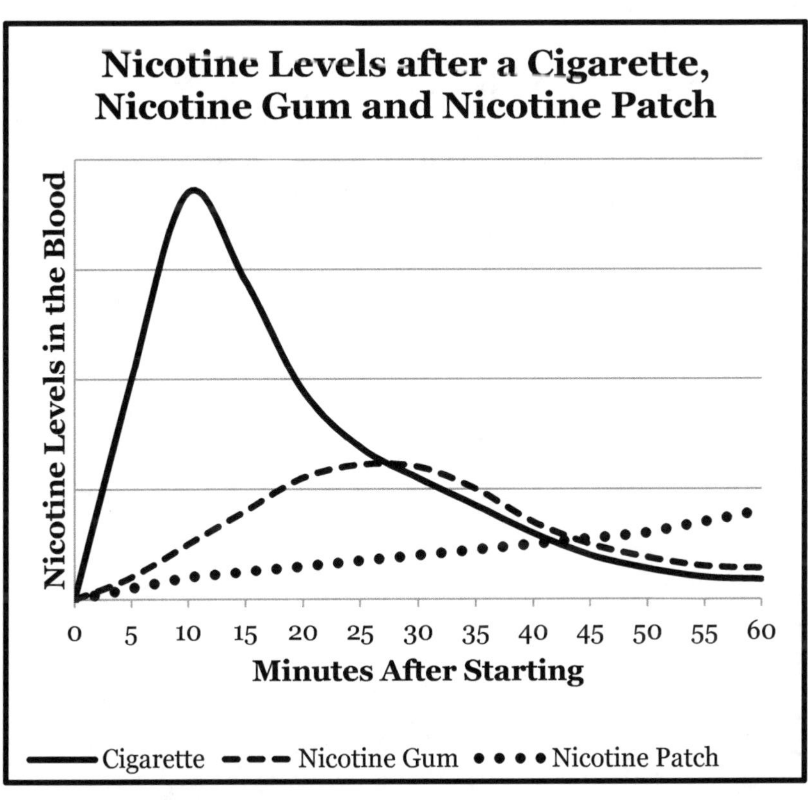

This figure compares the nicotine levels in the blood after smoking a cigarette compared to using the nicotine gum and patch. A cigarette produces a rapid spike in nicotine levels over just a few minutes. The gum produces much lower levels of nicotine, peaking after about 20-30 minutes. The patch takes about 4 hours to reach its maximum effect (not shown), but it is still far below what is produced by a single cigarette.

Smokers need not be worried about overdosing on NRT. The next figure shows nicotine levels in the blood over 24 hours. This illustration assumes that a person is wearing the 24 hour patch which produces steady blood levels all day and night. The figure shows that smoking produces very high levels of nicotine during the day and these fall to almost zero by morning. This up and down action makes it impossible for the brain to adjust.

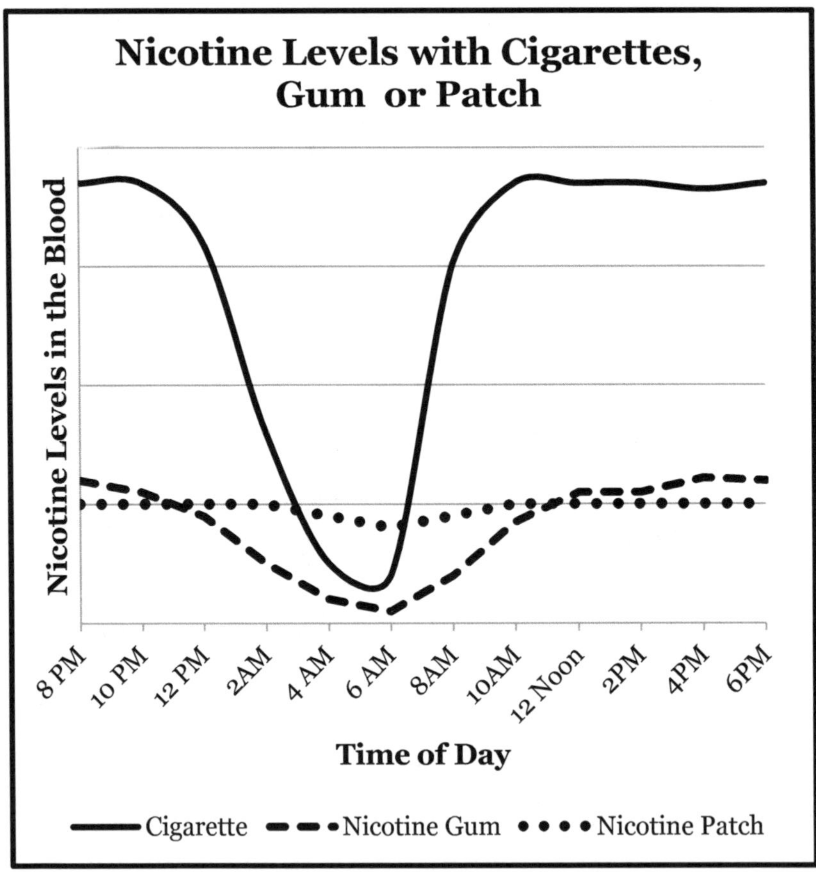

When tapering with NRT you have to give your brain plenty of time to adjust. Doctors do not yet understand what is going on in your brain that allows it to adapt to having less and less nicotine, but it probably involves growing new nerve connections. These things take time. The longer you give your brain to make these changes, the better the job it will do. Don't rush it.

You always want to be using enough NRT so you do not feel withdrawal symptoms, which includes craving for a cigarette. The purpose of NRT is to prevent withdrawal, not to rescue you from it when you can't take it anymore. Actually, NRT is lousy at rescuing people from withdrawal because it delivers nicotine so slowly. If you wait until you are in the grips of craving, it can take quite a while for NRT to relieve the craving. While a cigarette delivers a full dose of nicotine to your brain in 14 seconds, it takes the patch 4 hours to build up to its maximum dose. This is because the nicotine has to soak through the skin. Nicotine gum provides nicotine much faster than the patch, but it still takes 20 to 30 minutes to deliver its maximum dose. Also, as you can see from the figures, NRT provides much lower peak levels of nicotine than a single cigarette. So NRT will never provide the immediate relief from withdrawal that you are guaranteed with one cigarette.

The lesson here is that you have to stay ahead of withdrawal symptoms, just like you do when you are smoking. People wait too long to start NRT. They want to see how long they can go cold turkey before they use the NRT. They want to use as little NRT as possible. This is a recipe for failure. Before they know it, they are in severe withdrawal and at that point, NRT is too little too late.

Ordinarily you wouldn't wait until you absolutely need a cigarette before you smoke. You should never do that with NRT. At times you may light up a cigarette without even realizing it because your brain detects the first subtle signs of withdrawal and wants to head them off. When you are using NRT, you should be listening to the same signs you do when you smoke. What is the first thing you feel when it is time for a smoke? Do you have a mild desire? Do you find your concentration waning? Whatever it is, when you feel that, it is time for NRT. You need to nip those withdrawal symptoms in the bud and don't let them get any stronger.

For reasons that are beyond my understanding, smokers are afraid of NRT. This is ironic because all NRT products have been tested for purity, safety and effectiveness and cigarettes have not. The sad irony is that people on NRT who are feeling withdrawal symptoms may be afraid to increase how much they are using out of fear of overdosing on nicotine. So instead of using more NRT, they smoke a cigarette which gives them much higher levels of nicotine than they would ever get from NRT.

So smokers should not be afraid of NRT since the doses are low and since there are no reported cases of a smoker dying from an overdose of nicotine. If you want to see what an overdose of nicotine feels like, just smoke one cigarette after another until you start to feel sick. If you are taking NRT, and you do not feel like this, you are not taking too much. If you ever were to use too much NRT, you would feel like you did the first time you smoked a cigarette, a little nauseous and dizzy, that's all. Nobody has ever keeled over dead from a nicotine overdose from their first cigarette, and nobody has ever died from using too much NRT.

I have never encountered a smoker who took too much NRT, but if you start to feel nauseated and dizzy while taking NRT, just cut back a little. If a 12 year old can figure out how much of a cigarette to smoke without getting sick, you can figure out how much NRT you can use. After all, you are the expert. You adjust your nicotine levels every time you smoke. You know when you need more and when you have had enough.

Because smokers are leery of NRT products, they don't take a big enough dose to do them any good. If you want these products to work, you have to start by taking almost as much nicotine from the medicine as you would from smoking. If you are experiencing nicotine withdrawal symptoms like craving, you are obviously not using enough.

It is perfectly safe to put on a patch or two and use the nicotine gum at the same time. The biggest patch, the 21 milligram, provides about the same nicotine level as smoking a half a pack per day. But some people smoke two or three packs a day. That is like wearing 4 to 6 patches. When heavy smokers are in the hospital, we will put on two patches to keep them comfortable. A good strategy is to start with a patch and then use the nicotine gum throughout the day to keep those withdrawal symptoms away.

So how can you figure out what is the right combination of NRT for you? Before you quit smoking it might be helpful to do a few trial runs to see how much NRT it will take to keep withdrawal away. The patches have to be on your skin for three to four hours before they are delivering nicotine at their maximum rate. So one approach would be to put on a patch when you get up in the morning and then smoke as you ordinarily would throughout the morning. You will not die! Since you are getting some nicotine from the patch, you may find that you smoke fewer cigarettes than you usually would, or you will take fewer puffs from each cigarette, or you won't inhale as deeply. Your brain will automatically adjust your smoking so that you get the same level of nicotine in your brain as always.

After lunch, stop smoking and see if the patch alone will keep you from experiencing craving. If it doesn't, use the nicotine gum as often as you need to in order to keep the craving away for the rest of the day. You may need to chew the gum more often than you would usually smoke. Use as much NRT as you need to so that you are perfectly comfortable without smoking. If you are struggling and relying on your willpower, you are not using enough NRT. This is not a test to see if you can stop smoking; the goal is to find the right dose of NRT for you. If you need to smoke, smoke and try it again another day with a higher dose of NRT. If one patch wasn't enough, try two. Compared to cigarettes, all of the NRT products are weak and you have to use them aggressively if you want them to work for you. Play around with the NRT until you find the right combination that gets you through the rest of the day comfortably without smoking. Once you find the right dose for you, you can plan to include that in your strategy for quitting when the time comes.

When you quit with NRT, your first goal is to switch from cigarettes to a dose on NRT that is enough to keep you from feeling any withdrawal symptoms. Once your brain has gotten used to a steady level of nicotine on the NRT for a few weeks, then you can start tapering down on the NRT. One strategy is to wear a patch or two 24 four hours a day and then use as much gum as you need throughout the day to make sure you do not experience any craving. After you have done this for a few weeks, try to wean yourself down on the gum while you stay on the patches. After you are off the gum, you can wean yourself off the patches by using smaller patches.

I believe that when you quit cold turkey it takes your brain three months to fully adapt to life without nicotine. If you are weaning your brain off nicotine slowly, it may take even longer than three months for your brain to fully adapt. Nobody knows. But your brain is certainly not adapted after two or three weeks. Don't be in a hurry. Many people make the mistake of cutting back on NRT too quickly.

Suppose two buddies quit smoking together using NRT. One guy stopped using NRT after three weeks and the other is still using it after three months. If you had to bet, who would you bet would be an ex-smoker a year later?

I think most people would place their bet on the guy who got off of NRT after three weeks because that one seems less dependent. But actually, the longer people use NRT, the more successful they are at quitting because they give their brains plenty of time to fully adapt.

When you quit smoking using NRT, you should plan to use it for the full three months. Remember, when you use NRT you are NOT "replacing one addiction with another." You are gently weaning your brain off nicotine to cure your addiction. Don't scrimp on the cure.

NRT costs money and that is the main reason people try to scrimp. Let's compare the cost of smoking and the cost of NRT for a pack per day smoker. Let's start by assuming that a pack per day smoker would want to use one patch per day along with lots of gum, maybe as much as 15 pieces per day for the first month, 5 pieces per day for the second month, and none for the third month. This adds up to 84 patches and 560 pieces of gum. On the internet, at $2.40 each, 84 nicotine patches would cost about $200. At about 25 cents per piece, 840 pieces of nicotine gum would cost about $140. That adds up to $340 for a generous amount of NRT for three months. Now let's compare that to what our pack per day smoker would spend on cigarettes over three months. In 2010, the average cost of a pack of cigarettes was $4.80, or $403 for three months.

But your choice isn't between using NRT for three months or smoking for three months. You have to compare the cost of three months of NRT against what you will spend over the rest of your life on cigarettes if you don't stop smoking. At $4.80 per pack, smoking one pack per day adds up to $1,752 per year. If you were to smoke for another 10 years, it would add up to $17,520, assuming that the price never goes up. Trying to save a few dollars by scrimping on the cure for your addiction could end up costing you thousands of dollars in the future.

To review, the first mistake people make with NRT is not using enough to prevent withdrawal. The second mistake is not using it long enough. The third mistake is not using the gum correctly. If you don't use the gum correctly you may get very little benefit from it.

Here is an interesting fact for you. The nicotine molecule can exist is two forms depending on how much acid or alkaline is in its environment. (Alkaline is the opposite of acid.) Cigarette manufacturers add chemicals to cigarettes to put nicotine in a form that allows it to be absorbed very efficiently in the lungs. The nicotine in chewing tobacco and snuff is in a form that allows it to be absorbed very efficiently in the alkaline saliva of the mouth. The nicotine in cigar smoke is also in a form that allows it to be absorbed in the alkaline environment of the mouth. That is why you don't have to inhale cigar smoke to absorb the nicotine, you just have to hold it in your mouth.

Saliva is naturally alkaline and this aides the absorption of nicotine through the lining of your mouth. The nicotine in the gum is only absorbed well when you have saliva in your mouth. When don't you have saliva in your mouth? When you have washed it all down into your stomach by drinking.

When you drink a beverage like coffee, soda, or orange juice, you replace the alkaline saliva with acid. If you are chewing nicotine gum while you are drinking these acidic beverages, you may not be absorbing any nicotine. You have to wait 20 minutes after you finish one of these beverages before the nicotine from gum will do you any good. If you swallow too frequently when you chew the gum, the nicotine goes into your stomach where the acid there prevents it from being absorbed into your blood stream. To get the most out of the gum, you do not want to drink while you are using it and you don't want to be swallowing the nicotine because it does you no good in your stomach.

The package instructions tell you to chew the gum slowly, so the nicotine will be released slowly. But if you are having craving while you are chewing the gum, you are not getting enough nicotine and you may have to chew faster. This is something you should figure out when you are doing your trial runs to see how much NRT you need. You can chew one piece of gum all day, but after 20 to 30 minutes, depending on how fast you chew, you have used up the nicotine.

The gum comes in 2 mg and 4 mg strengths. Unless you are a very light smoker, I would get the 4 mg strength because you get more nicotine for your money. You can adjust how fast the nicotine is released by how fast you chew.

What if you have used NRT for 3 months and are still having cravings when you try to stop? You can continue NRT as long as you like, for a year, or the rest of your life. Only about 1% of smokers who use NRT have trouble stopping it. NRT is harmless, and it is infinitely better to chew the gum for the rest of your life than to smoke for the rest of your life if it came down to that.

In smoking cessation studies, NRT increases the rate of successful quitting by 70% for the gum and 95% for the patch. I think this underestimates how much help you can get from NRT if you use it right. The problem with these studies is that they did not try to determine the right dose for each person, they just put everyone on the same dose, and the dose was almost always too small since the subjects in these studies report lots of withdrawal symptoms. I believe you can do a lot better than those people because you now know how to figure out the right dose of NRT for you.

Bupropion

The prescription drug bupropion was the second type of medication approved for use in smoking cessation in the US. It has been on the market since the 1980's so its safety is very well established. Bupropion is sold as a generic drug and under the brand names of Zyban and Wellbutrin. Like many prescription drugs, bupropion has more than one use. Before it was approved for use as a smoking cessation drug, bupropion was (and still is) used as a treatment for depression. Bupropion works by changing the balance of chemicals in your brain in a way that reduces nicotine withdrawal symptoms. You have to start the medication a week before you stop smoking so that it has time to prepare your brain.

Most people tolerate this medication very well. To reduce the likelihood of side effects, you take just one pill (150 milligrams) per day for the first three days. After that you take a full dose of 150 mg twice a day. (There are also sustained release pills that you could take once a day.) After you have been on the medication for one week, it is time to stop smoking. The purpose of bupropion is to relieve withdrawal symptoms. For some people it works very well, but other people still experience withdrawal symptoms even while taking the medication. If you are taking bupropion and are having withdrawal symptoms you should also use NRT. If you tried quitting in the past with bupropion and had withdrawal symptoms, try it again with NRT. It is perfectly safe to use these two medications together. Sometimes withdrawal symptoms are so strong that you do need to go to double coverage to keep them in check.

You should stay on the bupropion for at least three months. You don't have to taper off of bupropion like you do with NRT. Some of my patients say that when they were on bupropion they noticed that they felt better than usual. This is because they were depressed before they quit smoking and the bupropion treated both their depression and their withdrawal symptoms.

Other patients tell me that after they stopped the bupropion they felt down. They thought that this might be a withdrawal symptom caused by stopping the bupropion, but actually these patients also had depression that the bupropion was treating. When they stopped the bupropion, their depression came back. If you feel better on bupropion than you do off of it, the only explanation is that you have depression.

When doctors use medication to treat depression, we treat for six months to a year. After that we stop the drug and wait to see if the depression returns. For some people, the depression is gone, but for other people, anytime they are off medication their depression comes back. These people benefit from staying on the drug indefinitely. There are people who have taken bupropion safely for decades. It is not addictive and has no long term side effects. You should have no concern about using it for the full three months to stop smoking and to remain on it for as long as you feel it is helping you. If you are still having craving after three months, ask your doctor to keep you on the medication longer.

The effectiveness of bupropion in helping people stop smoking has been demonstrated in dozens of studies. On average, bupropion increases the success rate by 210%.

Varenicline

The prescription drug varenicline is the third type of medication approved for smoking cessation. It was approved by the Food and Drug Administration in 2006. Varenicline is sold under the brand name of Chantix and the US, and Champix in Europe. The varenicline molecule fits into the nicotine receptors in the brain and stimulates them half as much as nicotine does. At the same time, it blocks nicotine from stimulating the receptors. By stimulating the receptors varenicline helps to reduce nicotine withdrawal symptoms.

Like with bupropion, you start to take varenicline one week before you quit smoking. The most common side effect with varenicline is nausea, but this usually goes away in a few days if you continue to take it. Cutting back on how much you smoke during the first week that you take the varenicline can also help to cut down on nausea. To cut down on the nausea, varenicline comes in a starter pack. The starter pack starts you off on one small pill each day for three days and then twice a day for four days. On day 8, when you are supposed to stop smoking, you graduate up to full strength pills twice a day.

While nausea is the most common side effect, it is usually mild and temporary and does not usually prompt people to stop the medication. The side effect that is most likely to cause people to stop varenicline is vivid dreams. People do not describe these as nightmares, they are just very vivid. This side effect does not appear to go away with continued use. If you get these dreams, before you give up on this medication you should try skipping the evening dose and take it only once a day in the morning. Sometimes this will stop the dreams.

While it is more common for people to stop varenicline than bupropion because of annoying side effects, varenicline is much more effective in helping people quit smoking. In studies, varenicline increases the success rate for smoking cessation by an average of 240%.

Because varenicline is the most effective medication for helping people stop smoking, it makes sense to try it first. If you don't tolerate varenicline, or if it doesn't work for you, try bupropion.

It is important to understand what these stop smoking medications do not do. They do not make you want to stop smoking. They do not make you sick if you continue to smoke. They do not block cue-induced urges to smoke, and they do not cure psychological dependence. They only help with withdrawal. This is why it is important that your defense strategy includes ways to deal with these other challenges.

Chapter 9
Choosing Your Game Plan

In the first book you learned all about nicotine addiction. You learned how Nicotine brought you from your first cigarette to the point you are at now. In this book you have learned about the three power players that stand between you and victory over your addiction to nicotine: withdrawal, cue-induced craving, and psychological dependence. Like a good quarterback, you have studied your opponent. You know its strengths and weaknesses. You have completed the questionnaires that helped you determine how much each of these players is going to be a challenge for you when you quit smoking. You have read about defensive strategies for dealing with each of these. A good quarterback doesn't go into the game with one play. He has dozens of plays ready. Now is the time for you to assemble your play book for the big game. In this chapter you will get to select your plays from the dozens of strategies we have already discussed.

A good quarterback does not go into a game cold, he prepares by practicing his plays with his team during the weeks leading up to the big game. As we go through these strategies, we will start with those that you should do before they day you will stop smoking. Sometimes quitting smoking is a team sport, you might need the cooperation and support of loved ones before you quit.

The first thing you need to do is to be sure quitting is what you want to do. Make your list of pros and cons and decide whether you want to quit or not. If you are not ready to quit, you might want to read the appendix for some scary inspiration.

The following pages list the strategies we have already discussed. As you go down these lists, check off the strategies you plan to use. The more, the better. If you made it less than a week the last time you tried to stop smoking, you were probably over powered by Withdrawal and you should plan to use Chantix, bupropion or NRT for your next attempt.

Strategies to use before you quit	Include in my playbook
Power player #1 Withdrawal symptoms	
Start varenicline a week before your quit date.	
Start bupropion a week before your quit date.	
If you are going to use NRT, do a few practice runs to find the right dose for you.	
Begin to work out to avoid weight gain.	
Plan a stress-free retreat for your first days of withdrawal.	
Power player #2 Cues	
Make your home and car permanent smokefree zones a few weeks before you quit.	
Break all of your smoking habits while you continue to smoke by changing up where and when you smoke.	
Remove reminders of smoking from your environment.	
Make a deal with your partner to quit together or not to smoke in your presence.	
Plan activities in places where smoking is prohibited.	
Power player #3 Psychological dependence	
Ask your ex-smoker friends and relatives if they can handle stress without smoking.	
Before you quit smoking, make yourself deal with stressful situations without smoking to prove that you can do it.	
Try hypnosis to give you confidence in your ability to cope.	

Strategies to use when you quit	**Include in my playbook**
Power player #1 Withdrawal symptoms	
Use varenicline	
Use bupropion	
Use NRT	
Use pain medications for headaches, and sleeping pills for insomnia.	
Keep yourself busy at all times.	
Recognize your withdrawal symptoms and remember that this is not your normal personality, it is withdrawal.	
Don't own the cravings. Remember that it isn't you that wants the cigarette, it's your brain.	
Actively ignore your brain when it is trying to tell you it wants a cigarette.	
Drown out the cravings by talking back. Give your &#*! brain a piece of your mind when it tells you it wants a cigarette.	
Don't listen to your brain. Distract yourself at the first sign of wanting or craving.	
Reread your list of reasons for quitting.	
Remind yourself that withdrawal is temporary. Focus on the light at the end of the tunnel.	
Power player #2 Cues	
Avoid being with people who smoke.	
Avoid situations where people will be smoking.	
Avoid situations that you associate with smoking.	
Avoid alcohol.	
Don't linger at the table after a meal.	

Power player #3 Psychological dependence	
Count each day without smoking as another victory, and keep score.	
At the end of each day, think of all of the stressful situations that you handled without smoking.	
Fill out the Autonomy Scale once a week so you can see your progress as your symptoms fade away.	

Once you have chosen your strategy, pick a date to quit and put your plan into action. If you have included a prescription medication in your strategy you will need to call or see your doctor. Health insurance usually pays for varenicline and bupropion, but not NRT since that is available without a prescription. Some states have programs that supply free NRT if you call their stop smoking program.

The Autonomy Scale

You have already filled out the Autonomy Scale (the AUTOS) in bits and pieces (the questions about withdrawal, cues and psychological dependence). Autonomy means freedom. The AUTOS measures the ways in which nicotine has taken away your freedom. When you quit smoking, your freedom from nicotine addiction comes back a little at a time.

Sometimes smokers get discouraged a week or two into quitting because they expected that they would no longer have any desire to smoke by this time. To give my patients a reason to be encouraged, I have them fill out the AUTOS before they stop smoking and then once a week after they stop. When they do this, they can see that the symptoms they are still dealing with are milder than they were when they were still smoking. They also see that some of the symptoms they had when they were smoking are gone completely.

The AUTOS is reproduced in its entirety on five consecutive pages. Fill out the first one now, before you quit smoking and then fill out the others once a week after you quit. By filling out the AUTOS each week, you can track how your symptoms of addiction disappear. This will give you some concrete evidence that you are slowly conquering your opponent.

If you add up your AUTOS score each week, you will see that the strength of your addiction will grow weaker and weaker until it is gone.

Complete the AUTOS before you quit.

The Autonomy over Smoking Checklist	Describes me...			
	not at all	*a little*	*pretty well*	*very well*
When I go too long without a cigarette I get nervous or anxious	1	2	3	4
When I go too long without a cigarette I lose my temper more easily	1	2	3	4
When I go too long without a cigarette I get strong urges that are hard to get rid of	1	2	3	4
When I go too long without a cigarette I get impatient	1	2	3	4
I would go crazy if I couldn't smoke	1	2	3	4
I rely on smoking to deal with stress	1	2	3	4
I rely on smoking to take my mind off being bored	1	2	3	4
I rely on smoking to focus my attention	1	2	3	4
After eating I want a cigarette	1	2	3	4
When I smell cigarette smoke I want a cigarette	1	2	3	4
When I see other people smoking I want a cigarette	1	2	3	4
When I feel stressed I want a cigarette	1	2	3	4

Complete this one week after you quit.

The Autonomy over Smoking Checklist	Describes me...			
	not at all	*a little*	*pretty well*	*very well*
When I go too long without a cigarette I get nervous or anxious	1	2	3	4
When I go too long without a cigarette I lose my temper more easily	1	2	3	4
When I go too long without a cigarette I get strong urges that are hard to get rid of	1	2	3	4
When I go too long without a cigarette I get impatient	1	2	3	4
I would go crazy if I couldn't smoke	1	2	3	4
I rely on smoking to deal with stress	1	2	3	4
I rely on smoking to take my mind off being bored	1	2	3	4
I rely on smoking to focus my attention	1	2	3	4
After eating I want a cigarette	1	2	3	4
When I smell cigarette smoke I want a cigarette	1	2	3	4
When I see other people smoking I want a cigarette	1	2	3	4
When I feel stressed I want a cigarette	1	2	3	4

Complete this two weeks after you quit.

The Autonomy over Smoking Checklist	Describes me...			
	not at all	*a little*	*pretty well*	*very well*
When I go too long without a cigarette I get nervous or anxious	1	2	3	4
When I go too long without a cigarette I lose my temper more easily	1	2	3	4
When I go too long without a cigarette I get strong urges that are hard to get rid of	1	2	3	4
When I go too long without a cigarette I get impatient	1	2	3	4
I would go crazy if I couldn't smoke	1	2	3	4
I rely on smoking to deal with stress	1	2	3	4
I rely on smoking to take my mind off being bored	1	2	3	4
I rely on smoking to focus my attention	1	2	3	4
After eating I want a cigarette	1	2	3	4
When I smell cigarette smoke I want a cigarette	1	2	3	4
When I see other people smoking I want a cigarette	1	2	3	4
When I feel stressed I want a cigarette	1	2	3	4

Complete this three weeks after you quit.

The Autonomy over Smoking Checklist	Describes me...			
	not at all	*a little*	*pretty well*	*very well*
When I go too long without a cigarette I get nervous or anxious	1	2	3	4
When I go too long without a cigarette I lose my temper more easily	1	2	3	4
When I go too long without a cigarette I get strong urges that are hard to get rid of	1	2	3	4
When I go too long without a cigarette I get impatient	1	2	3	4
I would go crazy if I couldn't smoke	1	2	3	4
I rely on smoking to deal with stress	1	2	3	4
I rely on smoking to take my mind off being bored	1	2	3	4
I rely on smoking to focus my attention	1	2	3	4
After eating I want a cigarette	1	2	3	4
When I smell cigarette smoke I want a cigarette	1	2	3	4
When I see other people smoking I want a cigarette	1	2	3	4
When I feel stressed I want a cigarette	1	2	3	4

Complete this four weeks after you quit.

The Autonomy over Smoking Checklist	Describes me...			
	not at all	*a little*	*pretty well*	*very well*
When I go too long without a cigarette I get nervous or anxious	1	2	3	4
When I go too long without a cigarette I lose my temper more easily	1	2	3	4
When I go too long without a cigarette I get strong urges that are hard to get rid of	1	2	3	4
When I go too long without a cigarette I get impatient	1	2	3	4
I would go crazy if I couldn't smoke	1	2	3	4
I rely on smoking to deal with stress	1	2	3	4
I rely on smoking to take my mind off being bored	1	2	3	4
I rely on smoking to focus my attention	1	2	3	4
After eating I want a cigarette	1	2	3	4
When I smell cigarette smoke I want a cigarette	1	2	3	4
When I see other people smoking I want a cigarette	1	2	3	4
When I feel stressed I want a cigarette	1	2	3	4

I am going to repeat something I said in a previous chapter. Your brain has one major vulnerability; its offense gets weaker over time. If you deprive your brain of nicotine it will desperately do whatever it can to get you to smoke a cigarette, but at the same time it is already making the necessary adjustments so that it can be in balance without nicotine. As your brain gets used to doing without nicotine, its offense gets weaker and weaker, and eventually it gives up. All you need to do to win is stay in the game. If you can refrain from smoking a single cigarette, you win.

What if you don't win? You have to figure out what went wrong. What tripped you up? Was it withdrawal, cues, psychological dependence, or something else? Whatever the reason, you have to improve your game plan to deal with it. If you tried one stop smoking medicine, try another. Try two at one time. If it was a certain situation that tripped you up, revise your game plan to avoid that situation, or come up with another way to handle it if it is unavoidable.

In surveys of ex-smokers, they say it took an average of five to six attempts to quit before they were finally successful. They learned something from those failures that helped them to eventually succeed. If you fail in your next attempt to stop smoking, learn something from that and come up with a smarter game plan.

If you are playing your friend at some game or sport and you lose you don't say, "You are better than me. I can't win." You say, "best out of three." You should have the same attitude with nicotine addiction. "OK, you beat me this time, but next time I'm going to kick your butt." The important thing to keep in mind is that nicotine addiction is a medical condition, it is not a test of your moral character or willpower. If at first you don't succeed, it does not mean that there is something wrong with you as a person. Give it another try.

Chapter 10
Snatching Defeat from the Jaws of Victory

Many smokers blow it in the last minute of the game. Once you are addicted to nicotine, there is always one more minute left on the game clock. The game is never over. You may enjoy a comfortable lead but it is never too late to blow it. Many smokers feel that once they are out of the woods and the cravings have long passed, they can enjoy an occasional cigarette now and then without getting addicted.

The story I hear from my patients over and over is that they were at a party drinking, having a good time, and someone else was smoking. The cues of alcohol, the sight of the cigarette and the smell of the smoke triggered a craving for a cigarette and they thought a few puffs wouldn't do any harm. But that one cigarette restored their addiction to full strength and a few days later they were back where they started.

Constant vigilance is the cost of freedom from nicotine. Never let your guard down. The game is never over. It doesn't matter if it has been three days since you stopped smoking, or three years. One cigarette can wipe out everything you have accomplished and restore your addiction back to its original strength. So don't go snatching defeat from the jaws of victory.

Chapter 11
Benefits of Quitting

You are never too old to benefit from quitting smoking. Your risk of getting a disease caused by smoking begins to decline the minute you stop smoking. Quitting smoking will add several years to your life expectancy. Within a few days of quitting smoking your risk of having a heart attack begins to go down. Within about two years, your risk of a heart attack will be the same as if you had never smoked.

Immediately upon quitting smoking, the irritation to your lungs stops. The inflammation, mucous and swelling in your airways diminishes. Within days you may notice that your breathing is a little easier. The hair cells that line your airways come alive again and begin sweeping the smoke particles from your lungs. You may notice that you cough up phlegm for a week after you quit as your lungs do a little spring cleaning.

Your risk of cancer begins to decrease after you quit. If you start to work out you may notice that your endurance improves quickly once you stop smoking. You wouldn't have noticed it, but smoking damages your sense of taste and sense of smell. Your sense of taste will return quickly and you will start to notice the subtle flavors that make eating a pleasure.

Immediately upon quitting smoking you will smell better to other people, but you won't notice this because your sense of smell may take years to return to normal. If you count how many years you have smoked, that is how many years it takes for your sense of smell to fully recover. You will know you are on your way when you notice for the first time that smokers smell bad.

At some point you will lose your tolerance to being exposed to noxious smoke and you will react to second hand smoke like a normal person. The smoke may give you a headache, irritated eyes, a sore throat, or chest congestion. You may find the smell offensive. Now you are truly an ex-smoker.

Chapter 12
Plan B

For 50 years the tobacco companies claimed that smoking was not addictive. Now they tell the jury that smoking is addictive, but anyone can quit if they want to. They argue that the only difference between smokers and ex-smokers is that smokers lack will power. Yes, it does take a lot of determination to quit smoking, but that is because addiction is so hard to overcome. Like most diseases there are mild cases and severe cases. Treatments that work well for mild cases may not work for severe cases. People with mild cases of nicotine addiction can be cured, but I don't think everybody can be cured of nicotine addiction. I think there are people with such severe cases of nicotine addiction that they cannot be cured with the medications we now have available. Our medications certainly do not work on everyone. Even varenicline, our most effective treatment, fails most of the time.

The fact that smokers differ in the severity of their addiction is one reason why some smokers succeed at quitting while others do not. Another reason is that not all smokers are created equal. Many suffer from various mental illnesses. Less than one quarter of American adults smoke, but about 90% of Americans with schizophrenia smoke. Smoking rates are also higher among people with depression and attention deficit disorder. If a person has any of these other issues, it is going to be that much harder to deal with nicotine addiction.

If you are one of those people who have tried everything and still can't quit, you should go to Plan B. If you can't cure your nicotine addiction, you should just accept it, and don't beat yourself up about it. That doesn't mean that you should just accept it that you will die prematurely from one of 30 different diseases caused by smoking. Not everybody can be cured of nicotine addiction, but I believe that everyone can be cured of smoking. If you accept it that you will need a daily supply of nicotine for the rest of your life, there is no reason it has to be from the deadliest possible source.

Take Care of Your Health

Uncontaminated nicotine is not harmful to you. You could use it every day and live a healthy life. Today nicotine is available in many different products, some are perfectly safe, and others are quite deadly. If you can't conquer your addiction to nicotine, then at least decide to get your nicotine from a safe source.

Cigarettes are by far the deadliest source of nicotine because the nicotine is delivered with over 4000 other chemicals deep into the lungs. These 4000 chemicals are then distributed throughout your body where they damage just about every organ and tissue. Cigars are just as deadly as cigarettes if you inhale the smoke into the lungs.

If you do not inhale, cigars and pipes are still probably the second most dangerous source of nicotine. The smoke contains just as many chemicals as cigarettes, but if you do not inhale, most of the damage to your body will be limited to the heart, lungs, mouth and nose.

Chewing tobacco and snuff are less dangerous than cigarettes, cigars and pipes because there are fewer chemicals involved. It is the burning of the tobacco that creates the 4000 chemicals. However, chewing tobacco and snuff sold in the US is fermented in a way that actually increases the amount of cancer causing chemicals. The main health concerns with these products are cancer of the mouth and the destruction of teeth.

All of these sources of nicotine are dangerous to various degrees because the nicotine is contaminated with chemicals that cause disease.

There are many healthy alternatives. All of the nicotine replacement products sold by pharmaceutical companies are safe to use for a lifetime. All of these products have undergone rigorous evaluation by government regulators in many countries and are guaranteed for purity and safety.

The tobacco companies have also begun to market nicotine in forms that should be much less dangerous than cigarettes, cigars, pipes and chewing tobacco. Examples are nicotine lozenges and strips. These products have probably undergone more extensive evaluation for consumer likeability than the pharmaceutical nicotine products. It is extremely doubtful that the tobacco companies have subjected them to any kind of health safety evaluation. Because these products cannot be regulated as drugs under US law, the tobacco companies do not have to demonstrate that these products are safe or pure.

It seems that there are new nicotine products appearing every day. There are nicotine inhalers, nicotine water, and nicotine toothpaste. The newest fad is the electronic cigarette. The idea behind the electronic cigarette is that it delivers nicotine without burning tobacco. In theory, a cigarette that delivered pure nicotine would be safe. There are many different manufacturers of electronic cigarettes that use different designs. None of these have been tested for human safety. Some deliver carbon monoxide, a poison, along with the nicotine. Nobody has tested all of these products to see what the smoker is actually inhaling. Most brands of electronic cigarette are made in China. In light of the many recent incidents in which Chinese manufacturers have put deadly chemicals in consumer products exported to the US, I would be very worried about using an electronic cigarette manufactured by a company I never heard of in China.

In any case, if you cannot cure your addiction to nicotine, you can still live a long and healthy life if you switch to a safer source of nicotine.

If you continue to smoke, there are things you can do to reduce your risk of dying from smoking. Heart attacks and strokes are two of the major ways smoking kills people. If you continue to smoke, you should try to eliminate anything else that would put you at risk for these diseases. See your doctor and make sure your blood pressure is good and your cholesterol is low. Ask your doctor if you should be taking an aspirin every day to prevent blood clots and heart attacks. If you smoke, it isn't hypocritical or futile to exercise. Exercise may benefit you more than it would a nonsmoker.

Take Care of Your Family's Health

Whether or not you are successful at stopping smoking, you should make your home smokefree. In adults, second hand tobacco smoke causes heart attacks, lung cancer, and asthma attacks. In children, second hand smoke causes asthma, bronchiolitis, bronchitis, pharyngitis, tonsillitis, ear infections, pneumonia and Sudden Infant Death Syndrome. It is also harmful to the fetus of pregnant women. Pets are also harmed by second hand smoke. So if you can't stop smoking, think about minimizing the harm to your family by making your home a smokefree zone.

Be a Good Role Model

When parents smoke, their kids are more likely to smoke. But studies show that even more important than the parents' smoking is the parents' attitude about smoking. If you can't stop smoking, you can still be a valuable role model for your children and grandchildren. Here's how.

Do not defend your "right to smoke." Be honest and tell them that starting to smoke was the stupidest thing you ever did. Tell them if they start to smoke, it will be the stupidest thing they will ever do. Tell them how disappointed you will be if you find out they did something so stupid as to start to smoke.

Never tell them that you enjoy smoking. Tell them you hate it, and tell them why.

Explain that you desperately want to quit, but you are addicted and the doctors' medicines won't work on you. Tell them that you are a very strong person, but addiction can be extremely hard to conquer.

Kids know that cigarettes are addictive, but none of them know what that means or feels like. Tell them what addiction feels like. Make it real for them. Tell them how unpleasant it is when you need a cigarette.

Show them the appendix to this book.

You don't have to quit smoking to be an anti-smoking crusader in your family.

Appendix

The Health Hazards of Tobacco Use

The purpose of this book is not to scare smokers into quitting. But some people say they want to be scared to help motivate them to quit. So, if you are interested, these are some of the diseases that are caused by smoking.

Most of the diseases caused by smoking appear after many years of smoking, but complications of pregnancy are an exception.

Smoking by either partner makes it more difficult for a woman to get pregnant. If a woman becomes pregnant, smoking makes it more likely that she will have a miscarriage. In these cases, smoking actually causes an abortion.

If the baby survives the early pregnancy, smoking increases the chances of it being born prematurely, underweight, or stillborn.

Because smoking puts a baby under stress during the pregnancy, the baby is more likely to die of infection during the first months of life, or from Sudden Infant Death Syndrome. Now that mothers are taught to put their babies to sleep on their backs, smoking during pregnancy is the main preventable cause of SIDS deaths.

If a mother smokes during her pregnancy and the child appears perfectly healthy throughout infancy, it is still at risk for mental problems. Nicotine affects the developing brain. Children who were exposed to smoking during pregnancy are 3 to 4 times more likely to develop Attention Deficit Hyperactivity Disorder. They are also more likely to develop delinquent behavior as a result of Conduct Disorder and Oppositional Defiant Disorder.

The 4000 chemicals in tobacco smoke are absorbed through the lungs and spread throughout the body.

In the skin and skeletal system smoking causes:

- premature facial wrinkles
- osteoporosis
- back pain

- leukemia

In the nervous system smoking causes:

- stroke
- cataracts in the eyes
- decreased sense of smell
- decreased sense of taste
- depression
- panic attacks

In the digestive system smoking causes:

- cancer of the lips
- periodontal gum disease leading to tooth loss
- mouth cancer
- throat cancer
- acid reflux
- esophageal cancer
- stomach ulcers
- stomach cancer
- pancreatic cancer
- cancer of the large intestine

In the respiratory system smoking causes:

- cancer of the nose
- cancer of the vocal chords
- emphysema
- chronic obstructive lung disease
- lung cancer
- bronchitis
- pneumonia
- wheezing
- collapsed lung
- stunted lung growth
- decreased stamina

In the circulatory system smoking causes:

- high blood pressure

- heart attacks
- ruptured aneurisms
- blockage in the arteries, leading to amputations
- blood clots in the legs
- fatal blood clots in the lungs

In the urinary system smoking causes:

- kidney cancer
- bladder cancer
- kidney failure

In the reproductive system smoking causes:

- erectile dysfunction
- infertility in males and females
- menstrual disorders
- miscarriage
- low birth weight
- premature delivery
- stillbirth
- premature menopause
- cervical cancer

Altogether, adding up all of these diseases, about half of all smokers die from diseases caused by smoking. That adds up to nearly 500,000 Americans each year. While it is true that everyone has to die from something, smokers tend to die from something on average about 8 years younger than nonsmokers. Not every smoker dies from smoking. Everyone seems to know a smoker who survived into their 80's. However there are also smokers who die 50 years younger than they would have if they hadn't smoked. Sometimes smoking combines with a strong family history of cancer or heart disease. I have had patients who have had massive heart attacks in their 20's from a combination of smoking and bad genes.

A lot of people think, if I smoke I might die 8 years younger, but all that I will miss is being elderly and frail. But that is not true. Even though they die younger, the average smoker has more years of sickness and disability than nonsmokers. Smokers become elderly and frail 8 years younger. Male smokers develop erectile dysfunction at a much younger age than nonsmokers. When people are asked to rate the ages of people in pictures, they judge 40 year old smokers to be the same age as 50 year old nonsmokers. By the time most smokers are 40 years old, they feel and look like they are 50 years old. Because smokers become sick and frail a decade earlier than they would have if they had not smoked, the years of life that they lose out on are the healthy years.

The good news is that quitting smoking at any age can add back some of those years.

About the Author

Joseph DiFranza is a family doctor and Professor at the University of Massachusetts Medical School in Worcester where he has been practicing medicine and conducting research on smoking for over 30 years. Dr. DiFranza was the first scientist to work out how nicotine addiction develops. He has published more than 150 scholarly articles on smoking and his Hooked on Nicotine Checklist is used in 18 languages around the world. In addition to his pioneering discoveries about nicotine addiction, Dr. DiFranza's research and advocacy played a key role in the elimination of the notorious Joe Camel cartoon ads, and the enforcement of laws prohibiting the sale of tobacco to minors.

Disclosure

The stop smoking medication Chantix is mentioned in this book. In the past, the manufacturer of Chantix, Pfizer, has awarded research funding to the University of Massachusetts Medical School to support Dr. DiFranza's neuroscience research. These research grants were awarded on the basis of peer-reviewed competitions. Dr. DiFranza does not accept speaking fees from drug companies. The preparation of this book was an independent personal project of Dr. DiFranza and received no support of any kind from Pfizer or the University of Massachusetts. All opinions expressed in this book are those of the author.